The Pillage
of the Third World

Pierre Jalée

The Pillage
of the Third World

Translated from the French by Mary Klopper

Modern Reader Paperbacks
New York and London

Preface to the English Edition

The Pillage of the Third World first appeared in France in the spring of 1965. It was revised a year later when some rather early figures were replaced by later ones and addenda were made to some chapters.

The English edition of the work will be published almost three years after its original appearance in France and it has, therefore, been necessary to bring the statistical aspect of it up to date as far as possible, by having recourse to the new data in the basic periodical publications which I had selected as reference works — most of which are United Nations publications.

There were two dangers attached to the work of revision: the first was that I might find figures in the statistical documents that were clearly more recent than those used in the two earlier French editions but which had been calculated on a different basis or grouped together in a different way. Such discontinuity might have made it difficult, or even impossible, to follow changes over a period long enough, and sufficiently recent, to provide a basis for conclusions. The second, more serious, danger was that I might encounter data which would invalidate or cast doubt upon certain statements or even whole theses which I had been bold enough to present.

The first difficulty appeared only with regard to movements of capital affecting the Third World (Chapter IV), concerning both public "aid" to the underdeveloped countries and private foreign investments made in them. My work in this field was based mainly on a United Nations booklet: "The International Flow of Long-term Capital and Official Donations" of which three editions had appeared dealing respectively with the periods 1951-1959, 1959-1961, and 1960-1962. One could observe considerable similarity among these three editions so that one could pass smoothly from one period to the next. In mid-1966 a fourth edition appeared dealing with the period 1961-1965 (really 1961-1964) which differed generally from the earlier ones, especially in the consistency and detailed nature of its statistical series. I was, therefore, faced with two alternatives: either to refer only to the latest edition which would have limited my observations to a recent but very short period and obliged me to reconstruct Chapter IV entirely; or to set the new document aside and remain on ground already explored, leaving a study covering a period of 10 to 12 years, up to and including 1962. I adopted the latter solution, in order to maintain the purpose of uncovering trends since these are significant only if shown over a period of time. I would certainly not have made this choice if the later figures had appeared to conflict with my earlier conclusions, but they do not even appear to modify them. I have also included some of the later figures as pointers. Perhaps it is not too early to mention here that I intend in a later work to take the most recent data it is possible to obtain and subject it to the further minute analysis which it requires. The figures one can assemble on this subject reveal an increasingly loose conception of "aid" to the Third World. It appears that various international agencies, conscious of the slow growth of assistance for the Third World, have been tempted to swell the total by including operations that can only be accepted by a stretch of the imagination: for example what in France is called "credit insurance" (official export credit guarantees).

In no case did I encounter the second difficulty I had feared: finding new figures which threw doubt on my earlier conclusions. I must, however, mention one point. In Chapter III, I noted that between 1948 and 1961 the exports of the industrialized capitalist countries to the Third World fell from 32 percent to 25 percent of their total exports inside the capitalist world. This fall in the relative importance of the Third World in the international trade of the imperialist countries has been interpreted by some observers as proof that the Third World has lost its former economic importance for imperialism which could with increasing ease afford to dispense with its trade with the underdeveloped countries. In the process of revision for the English edition I have learned that the above proportion has fallen to 23 percent. In the meantime I have, rather belatedly, read an article by the Marxist economist, Ernest Mandel, which appeared in the August-September 1964 issue of *Les Temps Modernes*. In this article Mandel tells us that "trade between the industrially advanced nations has more and more replaced trade between the underdeveloped world and the economically advanced world" and that, for this reason "the underdeveloped countries can, less and less, be used as a safety-valve for the capitalist system as a whole."

Even in the first edition of *The Pillage of the Third World* I expressed disagreement with similar suggestions (see pp. 53-55 of this edition). However, my disagreement with Ernest Mandel seemed to me so fundamental that I made it the main subject of two articles which appeared in *Partisans*, December 1965 and January 1966. Practical considerations have prevented me from elaborating on this point in the present edition. More recent data and what I believe to be a mistaken statement by a Marxist economist with a justly high reputation did not, in fact, make me change my views on the matter but, rather, spurred me to make a longer analysis in order to confirm them.

I feel that this question is so vital that it cannot be dealt with in haste. To correct a mistaken view which I believe to be harmful, it is necessary to sift the statistics and throw the most penetrating light on trade between the Third World and the imperialist countries on the one hand, and on trade among the different imperialist countries themselves on the other. This is too large a task to be undertaken within the time-schedule for the present publication. I will set about it in a later work. Meanwhile, I ask my English-speaking readers to pay special attention to the passages in this book cited above.

If I had had the opportunity to rewrite *The Pillage of the Third*

World instead of brushing it up — however conscientiously — I would, doubtless, have made a few more slight changes. Would Yugoslavia have remained on the list of socialist countries? The author is still in doubt on this point, and increasingly so. Would I not have placed more emphasis on the role of the United States of America as a super-imperialism? It seems likely. But, when all is said and done, it would not have been more than a matter of changing an emphasis here or there and, in no case, one of questioning my deductions or conclusions. On the contrary, as I continue to examine recent statistics and study new documents, I am confirmed in what I may presume to call the thesis of my work. English-speaking readers may rest assured that as I write these lines at the close of 1966, the basic ideas I held when I finished the first manuscript in 1964 have remained unchanged by two further years of investigation. I find myself, if possible, more firmly convinced of their soundness than ever before.

PIERRE JALEE

Paris
December, 1966

Contents

List of Tables

Introduction

The purpose of the present work is to examine the part played in the world economy by the Third World on the one hand and the industrialized capitalist countries on the other and, more especially, to illuminate the economic relations between the Third World and imperialism by following changes and trends in these relations.

The work is divided into six parts: the first chapter will set out the economic and political division of the world which has been adopted, and will give examples of the stages of development and rates of change in the different groups of countries which are to be considered. Chapter II will concern itself with problems of production, Chapter III with trade, and Chapter IV with movements of capital; in each case trends and changes will be followed as far as possible. Chapter V will make a special study of the convention associating eighteen African countries with the six countries of the European Common Market, for this contract has been taken as typical of neo-imperialist contracts. In a concluding chapter an attempt will be made to coordinate the major trends which have been revealed in the preceding chapters and, further, to set out certain perspectives that follow from them.

The work makes use of a great many figures and required the sifting of much statistical data. The source will always be given and will almost always be found in the documents of the United Nations.[1]

[1] In particular, the *United Nations Statistical Yearbook* and the *World Economic Survey,* both issued annually by the United Nations Department of Economic and Social Affairs, New York. The annual reports of the World Bank (International Bank for Reconstruction and Development) and its subsidiaries, the International Development Association and the International Finance Corporation, have also been used extensively. These are published by these bodies annually from Washington, D.C.

It seemed to me that this source would be the least open to question though I do not mean by this that data issued by the United Nations provide perfect material. United Nations documents have two disadvantages: one could sometimes wish that the figures were more recent; and they call for a certain amount of caution in making comparisons or grouping them together as they are not always calculated by identical methods or on an identical basis. But given this reservation, I think that United Nations figures can be accepted as orders of magnitude sufficiently significant for the particular purpose of making general comparisons, usually between groups of countries and only where major differences can be observed.

Some readers may be surprised to find me using, even in the title, the expression "Third World" of which I have been severely critical. This expression apparently came into use in 1956 and implies that the countries covered by it depend neither on the capitalist nor socialist system, that they belong to neither of the other two "worlds," which is obviously wrong. Many authors have, nevertheless, tried to maintain this thesis. We hear from Jean Lacouture and Jean Baumier that "in many respects the debate between capitalism and socialism seems out of date, at least in the Third World." [2] Give me but one example of a country which has escaped the dilemma!

The United States has an average national income of \$2,700 per capita and controls (even if with difficulty) the policy of half the world, a position that can surely not be equated with that of Morocco with a national income of some \$170 per capita. There can be no question of putting in the same category great powers and small underdeveloped countries, dominant economies and those which are dominated. The fact that imperialism entails an essential internal contradiction between exploiting countries and those that suffer exploitation does not destroy its unity; on the contrary, its unity is created by this contradiction without which it would not be imperialism. The United States, Britain, France, and a few others exploit the economies of 20 or 30 African countries for the benefit of monopolistic capital and they influence or control the policies of these coun-

---

[2] *Le Poids du Tiers Monde*, Paris, Arthaud, 1962.

tries to that end. All this does nothing to alter the fact that both groups are essential parts of the imperialist system — that is what makes imperialism what it is. On the other hand, although Morocco and Cuba present many common features which distinguish them clearly from the United States and France, there remains an essential difference between them: the one has maintained its links with imperialism and the other has broken them; the former depends economically and politically on one group of countries and the latter on the other — there is no third choice.

The so-called Third World is no more than the backyard of imperialism, which does not mean that it does not belong to the system — quite the contrary. The expression "Third World" does, however, tend to conceal this reality and it serves, objectively, to cause confusion.

The expression, however, found much favor: it is short, practical, and everyone knows pretty well what sort of country it refers to. Moreover, to group together the underdeveloped countries exploited by imperialism under a special heading implies, at least, that they compose a special area within the imperialist camp. This is almost to acknowledge in advance that their emancipation is inevitable and not too far distant in time. Having stated my reservations I will not persist in rejecting a term which, for better or worse, is universally used. Usage is paramount and I yield to usage.

Chapter 1

A World Sliced in Two

Geographically, the world is divided into five parts or continents but, politically and economically, I see it as essentially divided into two large units: (1) the group of countries which have chosen a socialist system, whether their socialism has been almost completely achieved or is still under construction, since the criterion is the decision taken in favor of a system based on Marxism-Leninism; (2) the group of countries which are still governed by the laws of the capitalist system.

In spite of major contradictions and ideological conflicts, the first group unquestionably presents an objective homogeneity because within it the socialist choice is nowhere questioned and appears to be irreversible. The doctrine common to the countries of this group provides the basis for relative unity of action on the major problems of the present era. It is unavoidable that differences have appeared and will appear among these countries, but they are contained within the uncontested framework of socialism and, in fact, arise directly from the search for better roads to socialism, better ways to build it or to defend it.

On the other hand, the second group of countries does not appear as a single unit and is, self-evidently, divided into two sub-groups: (a) The advanced capitalist nations, most of them highly industrialized, which comprise what is generally known as the imperialist camp or, more discreetly, the Western bloc; (b) The underdeveloped countries, whose economic and political structures are dominated by imperialism, and where the system of capitalist exploitation is generally most strongly opposed.

To make this study clear it is necessary at the start to state the composition of the groups of countries we have defined:

(1) *Socialist Group:* Soviet Union, European People's Democracies (including Yugoslavia), China, Mongolia, North Korea, North Vietnam, Cuba.

(2) *Capitalist Group:*

(a) *Imperialist Zone:* United States and Canada, Europe (excluding the Soviet Union and the People's Democracies), Japan, Israel, Australia and New Zealand.

(b) *Third World:* Latin America (excluding Cuba); the whole of Africa; Asia (excluding its socialist countries, Japan and Israel); Oceania (excluding Australia and New Zealand).

This economic and political division of the world is certainly open to question since some countries are near the borderline between groups or sub-groups and a few words of explanation may be useful:

(a) Yugoslavia is included among the socialist countries although one may have reservations about the socialist character of its policies, especially in the field of foreign affairs. I included it because I thought it right to give economics priority in making a classification and the economic basis of the Yugoslav system excludes private ownership of the means of production and the exploitation of man by man.

(b) One might be asked why, for instance, Cuba has been included with the socialist countries and not Algeria, which also calls itself socialist. This is simply because for me there is only one form of socialism — the socialism which is scientifically founded on Marxism-Leninism. Although Cuban socialism is still in its early stages it has given the strongest pledge of being irreversible by choosing such a foundation.

(c) I have included in the imperialist zone, as advanced capitalist countries, Southern European countries like Greece and Portugal, both of which are underdeveloped in certain respects. I think, however, that in many other ways they are firmly integrated with the group in which they are placed and simply constitute its poorest region. It is characteristic that Portugal has achieved the miracle of being both a colonizer and herself heavily colonized in the economic field, both underdeveloped and imperialist. But in the present world situation her colonialist and imperialist role is predominant.

Similarly, although Australia and New Zealand are mainly producers and suppliers of primary products, they are still essentially part of imperialism and might be described as an excrescence of that system projected to the other side of the world. On the other hand, although the productive system of South Africa has many features in common with the above two countries, and its white population has one of the highest standards of living in the world, it appears to me clear that it belongs in the Third World because its productive relations are based on the exploitation of an indigenous majority (four fifths of the population) by a resident colonizing minority. Like any other, this classification must needs be somewhat schematic, but I believe that it broadly reflects the basic political and economic divisions of the contemporary world. To give a precise conception of the relative sizes and populations of the different groups I have put together the essential data in Table I (p. 7).

The most striking feature of the table is the extent of the Third World countries and the size of their populations. They occupy slightly more than half of the world's surface and are inhabited by almost half (46.6 percent) of the world's population. Their territories are nearly double those of the advanced capitalist countries and their total population almost two and one half times that inhabiting those same countries. The estimated growth rate of populations must be treated with more caution than the other figures in Table I; nevertheless it appears certain that the rate of demographic growth is far greater in the Third World than in the advanced capitalist countries. My figures go back to 1964 and one may suppose that by now the Third World already holds a good half of the world's population

Table I

Population and Land Area in 1964

	Millions of inhabitants	Estimated annual population growth rate (%)	Area in 1,000 sq. km.	Density of Population per sq. km.
World	3,220	1.8	135,773	24
Socialist countries				
In Europe	121	1.0	1,273	95
U. S. S. R.	228	1.5	22,402	10
China	690	1.5	9,561	72
North Korea	12	3.0	121	98
North Vietnam	18	3.4	159	116
Mongolia	1	2.9	1,535	1
Cuba	7	2.1	115	65
	1,077 (33.4%)		35,166 (26%)	
Developed capitalist countries				
United States and Canada	211	1.7	19,340	11
Europe, excluding socialist countries	320	0.9	3,656	88
Japan	97	1.0	370	262
Israel	2	3.6	21	120
Australia and New Zealand	14	2.1	7,955	2
	644 (20%)		31,342 (23%)	
Countries of the third world				
America, excluding Cuba, the United States and Canada	230	2.8	22,608	10
The whole of Africa	303	2.4	30,258	10
Asia, excluding Japan, Israel, and socialist countries	963	2.2	15,844	61
Oceania, excluding Australia and New Zealand	3	2.8	555	6
	1,499 (46.6%)		69,265 (51%)	

Source: U. N. Statistical Yearbook, 1965, Tables 2 and 19.

and two and one half times that of the advanced capitalist countries. Before the end of the century the proportions will surely reach two thirds of the world's population and three times that of the advanced capitalist countries unless the Third World in the meantime loses some of its members to the socialist group.

There is already an extensive literature on the problems of underdevelopment. One of the best works on this subject is by Yves Lacoste: *Les Pays Sous-développés*.[1] The author selects no less than fourteen characteristics of underdevelopment, not all, of course, of equal importance. Two thirds of the inhabitants of the underdeveloped countries of the Third World do not get the essential minimum of 2,500 calories per day; the expectation of life for many of them is less than half that in the highly developed countries. Having reminded our readers of these most tragic aspects of underdevelopment I want to pick out a few indices which enable me to assess fairly accurately what differentiates the economically backward countries of Asia, Africa, and Latin America from the advanced capitalist countries. In Table II (p. 9) I have also set out four criteria of economic and social development, applied to four groups of countries: six of the major advanced capitalist countries, and three groups of five countries typical of Asia, Africa, and Latin America, respectively. From this table one sees that the people of Asia and Africa enjoy on the average one twelfth to one tenth, and those of Latin America a little more than one fifth, of the national per capita income of the people of the advanced capitalist countries. The disparities are also gross if one looks at the number of inhabitants per doctor even though one must preserve a little caution about some of the figures taken from United Nations statistics.

The most characteristic indices of economic development are the average per capita consumption of energy and industrial steel. These two indices vary from group to group studied in almost exactly parallel fashion. Broadly speaking, the countries of Asia consume per capita one sixteenth to one twentieth of the energy and industrial steel

---

[1] *Que Sais-je?* series, Paris, Presses Universitaires de France, 1962.

Table II

Indices of Development and Underdevelopment

Country	Per capita national income in dollars*		Per capita consumption, 1964 Energy in kgs. of coal or equivalent	Per capita consumption, 1964 Industrial steel in kgs.	Number of inhabitants per doctor 1960-1963
United States	1964:	2,700	8,772	615	690
United Kingdom	1964:	1,365	5,079	438	840
Federal Germany	1964:	1,415	4,230	579	670
France	1964:	1,370	2,933	356	870
Italy	1964:	760	1,659	221	610
Sweden	1964:	2,025	4,320	623	960
Averages for group**		1,605	4,500	470	775
Pakistan	1963:	80	86	11	7,000
India	1963:	80	161	16	5,800
Federation of Malaysia	1963:	235	373	43	10,500
Thailand	1963:	95	106	13	7,600
Iraq	1963:	210	666	28	4,800
Averages for group**		140	280	22	7,140
United Arab Republic	1961:	130	321	24	2,500
Morocco	1964:	170	149	16	9,700
Zambia	1964:	195	431	22	8,900
Nigeria	1962:	90	38	6	34,000
Ghana	1964:	250	120	11	12,000
Averages for group**		165	210	16	13,420
Peru	1964:	235	602	24	2,200
Argentina	1964:	685	1,242	93	670
Brazil	1960:	130	364	43	2,700
Chile	1964:	445	1,078	74	1,800
Colombia	1963:	230	494	31	2,000
Averages for group**		345	755	53	1,875

*Figures calculated by the author from data and conversion rates supplied in the United Nations Statistical Yearbook.

**These averages are simple averages.

Source: United Nations Statistical Yearbook, 1965.

consumed in the advanced capitalist countries, the countries of Africa consume only one twentieth to one thirtieth of that amount, and the countries of Latin America one sixth to one ninth. These figures give a very clear indication of the lack of industrialization in the countries of the Third World, and bear witness to the disequilibrium of their economies.

As was pointed out in the introduction, these figures must be regarded only as orders of magnitude. Per capita national income, in particular, is given for 1964 for the advanced capitalist nations but for earlier years for the nations of the Third World, so it is possible that the 1964 figures would be slightly less unfavorable to them.

Fully aware of certain imperfections, I believe that my comparative data provide realistic approximations which enable one to appreciate clearly what a gulf lies between the Third World and the advanced capitalist nations in general.

The data in Table II also provide a measure of the relative underdevelopment of the countries of the Third World in relation to each other. The criteria chosen show that among the groups of countries studied, Asia and Africa are the most underdeveloped. Latin America, on the other hand, is at a more advanced stage of development. Its per capita national income is more than twice that in Africa or Asia and its consumption of energy and industrial steel indicates the beginnings of some kind of industrialization. It is notable that the per capita consumption of energy in Argentina is not so very much lower than in Italy. Nevertheless, Latin America displays the essential features of an underdeveloped region. According to Carlos Fuentes, Latin American capitalism was —

superimposed on the feudal structure without destroying it. It abandoned to their fate the great masses of peasants and workers, and reserved progress for an urban minority. It ended by crystallizing a dual society in Latin America: the modern capitalistic society of cities and the feudal society of the countryside. The minority society became richer at every turn, face-to-face with a majority society becoming more miserable at every turn. . . . At present, 4 percent of the Latin American population receives 50 percent of the combined national incomes.[2]

One asks oneself whether the countries of the Third World, all underdeveloped, even if unequally so, are catching up, however slowly, with the level of development of the industrialized capitalist countries. Table III (p. 12) shows that they are not. It compares three groups of countries, socialist, capitalist, and Third World, showing changes in the gross national product per capita over the twelve years from 1953 to 1964, on the basis of an index of 100 for the year 1958, and at constant market prices. This table gives an approximate but useful scale of average economic growth by groups of countries, from which we can draw the following conclusions:

(a) The average growth of the socialist countries is about 57 percent higher than that of the advanced capitalist countries.

(b) The average growth of the advanced capitalist countries is more than twice that of the countries of the Third World.

It appears, therefore, that despite any errors or inadequacies, the socialist system has proved its clear superiority over the capitalist system in the matter of economic growth. But the most striking thing is the tragic slowness of economic growth in the thirteen sample countries from the Third World, taken over the period of twelve years, which makes it possible to assess a trend. Had it been possible to find information about more African countries in the United Nations data (only three are included in my Table) this lack of economic growth would doubtless have appeared even more striking.

Available figures for the last twelve years show that, in the conditions prevailing during that period, the gap between the level of economic development of the Third World countries and that of the industrialized capitalist countries has not narrowed but actually grown wider. The era of political decolonization has not been one in which the ex-colonies or dependent nations have victoriously pursued their

---

2 *Whither Latin America?,* New York, Monthly Review Press, 1963, pp. 11-13. A different view of the nature of exploitation in Latin America is presented by Andre Gunder Frank in *Capitalism and Underdevelopment in Latin America,* New York, Monthly Review Press, 1967, pp. 221 ff. and *passim.*

Table III

Changes in the Index of Per Capita Gross Domestic Product at Constant Prices
(1958 = 100)

	Index 1953	Index 1964	Changes over 12 years	Average of Changes
Socialist countries				
U. S. S. R.	65	134	69	
Bulgaria	82	169	87	
Czechoslovakia	75	118	43	
Hungary	84	141	57	69.4
Poland	73	127	54	
Roumania	79	168	89	
Yugoslavia	74	161	87	
Advanced capitalist countries				
United States	101	117	16	
Canada	98	114	16	
Japan	77	191	114	
United Kingdom	92	119	27	
Federal Germany	75	131	56	
France	84	126	42	44.1
Italy	80	136	56	
Sweden	88	130	42	
Belgium	91	129	38	
Netherlands	87	127	40	
Norway	91	129	38	
Third world countries				
Argentina	86	100	14	
Brazil	87	113 (1963)	28	
Burma	91	116	25	
Ceylon	99	101	2	
Colombia	92	113 (1963)	23	
India	95	112	17	21.7
Mexico	80	117	37	
Pakistan	102	118	16	
Uganda	97 (1955)	105	9	
Southern Rhodesia	89 (1955)	104	17	
Venezuela	81	109	28	
Thailand	99	127 (1963)	31	
Zambia	96 (1955)	126	35	

Source: United Nations Statistical Yearbook, 1965, Table 179. Where the figures in the Yearbook did not
cover the 12-year period from 1953 to 1964 (for certain Third World countries), the 12-year
change has been extrapolated from figures given.

former colonial masters or dominant nations; their economic backwardness is growing more severe and this situation calls for reflection and further study.

Most of the underdeveloped countries of Asia and Africa were until recently under the colonial system, directly controlled and administered by Western metropolitan powers, and few would now dispute that this entailed the exploitation of the wealth of these colonies and dependencies for the more or less exclusive benefit of the metropolitan powers which lay at the heart of imperialism. Many, however, have jumped to the conclusion that the political decolonization which is now under way, leads almost automatically to economic disengagement. It is more widely believed than may appear that the ex-imperial countries can more and more easily dispense with the profits once extracted from their former colonies and that they are doing so in practice. From this it is only a step to the more or less consciously racist concept that the increasing relative economic backwardness of the Third World is due to some congenital incapacity in "those countries."

On this question of the growing economic inequality between different groups of nations the United Nations World Economic Survey gives figures which differ considerably from those given in Table III. This United Nations document (see Table III-a, p. 14) gives the average rate of growth of the per capita gross national product, over the period 1950 to 1960, as 2.7 percent for the advanced capitalist countries, and 2.2 percent for the developing countries. This gap is notably less than that shown in our Table III. There seem to be two major reasons for the discrepancy:

(a) Different methods of calculation (especially simple averages in the first case and weighted averages in the second) and different periods covered (1953-1964 on the one hand and 1950-1960 on the other).

(b) The inclusion in Table III-a, under the heading "developing nations," of the sub-section "other countries" composed of nations which do not belong to our Third World and whose higher growth rate raises the average for the group.

Table III-a

**Per Capita Gross Domestic Product for Major Regions,
and Rates of Growth, 1950 and 1960**

	Amounts in 1960 dollars		Average annual rates of growth from 1950 to 1960 (%)
	1950	1960	
Developed countries with market economies	**1,080**	**1,410**	**2.7**
North America	2,340	2,718	1.5
Western Europe	655	946	3.7
Japan	193	418	8.0
Oceania and South Africa	800	948	1.7
Developing countries with market economies	**106**	**130**	**2.2**
Latin America	252	300	1.8
Africa	93	113	1.9
Far East	69	85	2.3
Western Asia	164	214	2.7
Other countries*	319	472	4.0

*This heading covers mainly the more backward European countries.

Source: United Nations World Economic Survey, 1963, Part 1, extracted from Table 2-3.

However this may be, the two sets of figures show the same trend clearly enough to put its direction beyond question. Moreover, the *World Economic Survey, 1963* (p. 21) adds an unequivocal commentary to the figures given: "With regard to per capita production, the gap between the two groups of countries with market economies has grown wider, not only in absolute value . . . but also in relative value. In 1950, production per capita was about ten times greater in the advanced regions than in the developing regions, and in 1960 it was eleven times greater."

Chapter II

Imperialism and the Third World:
Production Relations

In this study there will often be occasion to refer to the advanced capitalist countries which, in the previous chapter, were classified as sub-group (a) of those countries living under the capitalist system. For convenience, they will be referred to as "imperialist countries" or "imperialism," which is brief and reflects reality. It would not be correct to confine the concept of imperialism only to those countries which have had colonial empires or directly dominate a group of economically and politically dependent countries (for instance, the United States in relation to Latin America). Imperialism is even more clearly an economic phenomenon, implying certain relationships in the international division of labor, in trade and the movement of capital. Countries like Sweden and Switzerland, which have never had a colony or dominated one underdeveloped country more than another are, nevertheless, qualitatively as much imperialist as the United States or Great Britain; they are only quantitatively rather less imperialist and the increasing internationalization of oligopolistic and monopolistic capitalism makes it difficult to measure the extent of the difference.

The object of the present chapter is to assess the part played in the major fields of world production by the imperialist countries and those of the Third World respectively, and to seek to show the dependent relations that follow from the facts. It should be said at once, however, that useful as the examination of data relating to production may be, it cannot be fully appreciated unless considered in conjunction with other data, especially that concerning trade (see Chapter III).

Extractive Industries

As a general measure of the respective part played in the extraction of mineral wealth by the imperialist countries and the Third World, I have been able to find nothing better than a table of percentages of the total value added in the extractive industries in 1958. From this I was able to derive Table IV.

Table IV

Production of Extractive Industries of Non-Socialist World
(As Percentage of Total Value Added in 1958)

Regions	All extractive industries	Coal	Metalliferous minerals	Crude oil and gas
Africa and the Middle East	13.5	1.1	26.9	17.1
Latin America	8.4	0.6	13.3	12.4
Asia, excluding Japan and socialist countries	4.7	2.7	5.0	6.4
Total for group	**26.6**	**4.4**	**45.2**	**35.9**
United States and Canada	44.6	20.7	34.5	61.3
Europe, excluding socialist countries	25.5	67.1	15.2	2.7
Japan	2.2	6.3	2.6	0.1
Oceania	1.1	1.5	2.5	—
Total for group	**73.4**	**95.6**	**54.8**	**64.1**
Total for world, excluding socialist countries	100.0	100.0	100.0	100.0

Source: United Nations Statistical Yearbook, 1962, Table II.

The two groups of countries shown in Table IV approximate very closely the groups of Third World countries and advanced capitalist countries as previously defined. The data suggests that, by 1958, the production of the Third World was already more than one third that of the imperialist countries. Their production was very low in coal but considerably higher in oil and gas, and most of all in the metalliferous ores. That was all in 1958. According to Table 9 (II) of the *United Nations Statistical Yearbook, 1965,* the indices of production in the extractive industries, taking 1958 = 100 as a base, rose from 77 in 1948 to 119 in 1965 (nine months) for the industrialized countries (plus 42) and, over the same period, from 45 to 197 (plus 152) for those countries which the United Nations calls "less industrialized" and which are, in general, those of the Third World. These figures show a marked increase for the Third World in this field. The production of the Third World rose by 97 percent between 1958 and 1965 while that of the imperialist countries rose by only 19 percent. On this basis one can calculate that in 1965 the Third World provided 37.5 percent of the production of the extractive industries of the non-socialist world and the imperialist countries 62.5 percent. It can be seen that the respective contributions have changed greatly over seven years and it can be assumed that the change was especially marked in the sectors of oil, natural gas, and metalliferous ores.

The United Nations statistics show that in the field of crude oil the Third World countries have caught up with the imperialist countries, producing 700 million tons out of a world total of 1,410 million, while the imperialist countries were only extracting 450 million tons of which 377 million came from the United States alone.

With regard to iron, the position of the Third World is still weak, having only 25 percent of world production to its credit, but it is strong or very strong in the field of most of the non-ferrous mineral ores, as can be seen from the following figures (given in metal content):

In 1964 world production of copper ore (excluding China and the USSR) consisted of 4,220,000 tons, of which the Third World countries contributed 2,200,000, that is, more than half. Their position was even stronger in the production of manganese ore of which they produced 3,085,000 tons out of a total of 6,600,000 for the world (excluding China), or 3,400,000 after subtracting the Soviet Union's vast contribution of 3,200,000 tons. The Third World is also very fortunate in the production of cobalt; three African countries (Congo-Leopoldville, the ex-Federation of Rhodesia and Nyasaland, and Morocco) contributed 10,720 in 1964 out of a world (excluding the USSR) total of 14,900 tons. A similar situation exists for chrome ore and tin: in 1962, production of the former in the non-socialist world amounted to 1,260,000 tons, of which 930,000 came from the Third World (400,000 of which were from South Africa). In 1964 the Third World produced 142,000 tons of the total of 149,500 of tin concentrate for the world (excluding the USSR) and 17 million of the 29 million tons of bauxite extracted in the world (excluding USSR and China).

The strangest case of all, however, is that of antimony ore which in 1964 was almost entirely produced in the socialist group of countries (26,740 tons, including 15,000 tons from China) and in the Third World (33,000 tons). The world total was 64,000 tons.

In 1964 one quarter of the zinc ore and one third of the lead ore produced in the non-socialist world came from the Third World: 820,000 tons of the former and 610,000 tons of the latter. The metalliferous ores can be left with the observation that South Africa alone produced seven tenths of the world's gold.

Turning to other valuable products of the sub-soil, it might be mentioned that in 1961 three African countries between them produced 70 percent of the world's diamonds (Congo-Leopoldville 50 percent, and 10 percent each from South Africa and Ghana). In 1964 almost all the natural phosphates in the non-socialist world came from the United States which produced 23,330,000 tons, and the Third World which produced 19,500,000 tons (more than half of which came from Morocco, where production is still increasing rapidly). However, as United States agriculture consumes almost the whole of that country's production, the Third World is the major partner in world trade in phosphates.

From the above enumeration it can be seen that the "proletarian nations" are not poor because of a curse of nature, that they are not lacking in natural wealth, least of all in raw materials for heavy industry. They are poor only because, as we shall see, this natural wealth has been, and still is being, plundered by imperialism for the needs of its own industrialization, at the expense of those countries from which it flows away in its raw state.

It must be pointed out that the continued and increasing exploitation of the Third World by imperialism has positive aspects as well as negative ones. It is striking, for example, that the extractive industries of the imperialist countries grew by only 19 percent between 1958 and 1965, considerably less than other sectors of their industry. This is probably because deposits in these countries are becoming poorer, or unpayable, or inadequate to meet growing demand. At the same time the workings of the Third World are increasing in size and number (plus 97 percent from 1958 to 1965). Moreover, the imperialist zone is predominant in coal, which is a declining source of energy, while the relative position of the Third World is constantly improving in the production of oil and metalliferous ores. Imperialism exploits the subterranean wealth of the countries which it dominates because its industries require these materials but, for this very reason, the Third World has an ace up its sleeve; its hand is on the tap controlling an essential flow, and thus it enjoys a position of strength in one respect which must not be underestimated in a dynamic and changing world.

Manufacturing Industries

I have drawn up a table similar to Table IV for the extractive industries; it is derived from the same source and also relates to the year 1958 (see Table V, p. 20).

As might have been expected, the Third World is very much further behind the imperialistic countries in secondary industry than in the extractive industries. Almost half the world's population (that of the Third World) has only about one thirteenth the industrial pro-

Table V

**Production of Manufacturing Industries of Non-Socialist World
(As Percentage of Total Value Added in 1958)**

Regions	All industry	Light industry	Heavy industry
Africa and the Middle East	1.5	1.7	1.2
Latin America	3.7	5.3	2.7
Asia, excluding Japan and socialist countries	2.1	3.5	1.1
Total	7.3	10.5	5.0
United States and Canada	49.9	47.5	51.5
Europe, excluding socialist countries	37.6	36.6	38.2
Japan	3.5	3.5	3.7
Oceania	1.7	1.9	1.6
Total	92.7	89.5	95.0
Total (world excluding socialist countries)	100.0	100.0	100.0

Source: United Nations Statistical Yearbook, 1965, Table 11.

duction of one fifth of the world's population (the inhabitants of the advanced capitalist countries). In the key sector of heavy industry the disparity is even greater (one nineteenth instead of one thirteenth).

Can one at least discern a tendency, similar to that for the extractive industries, which suggests a progressive narrowing of the gap? The same Table 9 (II) of the *United Nations Statistical Yearbook, 1965*, shows us that on the base 1958 = 100, the index for the manufacturing industries of the industrialized countries rose from 62 in 1948 to 157 in 1965 (plus 95); over the same period the index for the "less industrialized" rose from 54 to 163 (plus 109). The difference in the growth rate is minimal. The figures in Table V, then, pretty closely approximate the respective share of the Third World and the imperialist countries in the industrial production of the non-socialist world in 1965, though the figures pertain to 1958. The total relative gap between the two groups is almost stationary. If one takes into account, however, that the population of the Third World is growing far more rapidly than that of the imperialist countries, one can see that the situation is not stationary but that the first group is falling behind the second as regards industrial growth per capita.

The serious nature of this situation can be better appreciated when it is remembered that one of the worst troubles of the Third World is not unemployment in the European sense, but "non-employment," and that experts generally place great reliance on industrial development to provide vast new employment opportunities.

To cast further light on this dramatic aspect of the underdevelopment of the Third World let us look at changes in employment indices (base 1958 = 100) in manufacturing industry (Table VI).

Table VI

Indices of Industrial Employment for Manufacturing Industry
(1958 = 100)

	1948	1963	Difference
World	**79**	**117**	**38**
Industrialized countries	83	113	30
United States and Canada	97	107	10
Europe, excluding socialist countries	80	111	31
(EEC only)	73	111	38
Less industrialized countries	72	125	53
Latin America	83	107*	24
East and Southeast Asia	70	132	62

*This figure applies to the year 1961.

Source: United Nations Statistical Yearbook, 1965, Table 11.

It is true that the industrial employment index rose faster for the "less industrialized" group than for the industrialized countries as a whole, but the difference between plus 53 and plus 30 is not much over a period of 16 years. Moreover, a comparison of the rates of progress of the index in the United States and Canada on the one hand, and in other industrialized countries on the other, shows that they are slower where industrialization is very advanced (effect of a high technical level, and of automation).

The lag of the Third World in the growth of manufacturing industry can thus be seen to be startling; there has been scarcely any reduction of that lag during the last 17 years, which suggests that under existing conditions it is beyond remedy.

There are no reliable figures for the Third World as a whole which measure the extent of foreign economic intervention but it is certain that many, perhaps even most, of the industrial undertakings of the underdeveloped countries are foreign-owned or controlled. Very often they are not appropriate to the needs of balanced expansion, and make only a minor contribution to primitive accumulation for growth since the greater part of the profits derived from them are repatriated (see Chapter IV). Such enterprises rarely fit into the development plans of the countries in which they operate; they are simply foreign enclaves placed there to extract surplus value.

In the early stages there may appear certain elementary industrial processes such as the enrichment of ores or the primary smelting of metals. In 1964 the Third World produced 255,000 tons of zinc from a total extraction of 820,000 tons of metal-bearing ore, and 385,000 tons of lead from a total extraction of 610,000 tons of metal-bearing ore. The metal ingots produced do not, however, feed local processing plants but are exported like the ores, and have only been smelted locally because freight charges make it advantageous to imperialism.

It would be interesting to establish for a whole range of basic industrial products what share of their own total production is utilized industrially in the countries of the Third World. I can give only two examples:

It was seen that in 1964 the Third World supplied 142,000 tons of tin concentrate out of a world production of 149,500 tons (excluding the USSR). During the same year its own industrial consumption was only 16,350 tons or 11.5 percent of its production.

In the same year that same Third World extracted 17 of the 29 million tons of bauxite produced in the world (excluding the USSR and China); that is, 59 percent of the total. This bauxite made possible the 1964 world production of 4,920,000 tons of aluminum (excluding the USSR and China) but only 150,000 tons or 3 percent was produced by the Third World for its own use.

Agriculture

As far as I know, there are no figures for agriculture, similar to those for industry, which would make it possible to relate total production of the Third World to that of the imperialist countries.

There are, however, indices of agricultural production by major regions so that we can compare growth rates in the two groups (Table VII, p. 24).

The second group of four regions is very close to the Third World as defined for this study, save that Japan is apparently included among the Far East countries. Thus one can say that over a period of several years agricultural production grew faster in the Third World than in the United States and Canada but slightly more slowly than in Western Europe. Since the United States, with its huge accumulated agricultural surpluses, is a special case, Western Europe provides a better norm for comparison. On this basis one can suggest that in absolute total, agriculture is developing along parallel curves in the Third World and in the advanced imperialist countries.

Unfortunately, this does not hold if one looks at per capita agricultural production, owing to the much faster rate of population growth in the Third World. Agricultural production per capita is declining in the Third World, is stable in North America, and increasing in Western Europe. This suggests that the problem of world hunger, that is, hunger in the Third World, is nowhere near a solution, since each inhabitant of the Third World has access to a shrink-

Table VII

Indices of Agricultural Production, 1964
(1958 = 100)

Regions	Index of total agricultural production	Index per capita
(a) Western Europe	116	109
United States/Canada	109	100
(b) Latin America	110	93
Far East (excluding China)	115	101
Near East	115	99
Africa	117	100
Simple average (Group b)	114	98

Source: United Nations Statistical Yearbook, 1965, Tables 5 and 6.

ing supply of agricultural produce (leaving aside gifts in the event of famine or disaster).

This appears to be the more serious when one estimates the preponderance of the agricultural population in the Third World: the work of by far the greater part of its people is bringing no relative progress — on the contrary, its results are actually declining. Table VIII (p. 25) gives some data on the relative size of the agricultural population in some major regions of the world.

So far, however, only overall agricultural production has been examined, but that of the Third World falls into two classes: (a) major basic food products or raw materials which are almost all exported to the advanced capitalist countries and (b) products for food consumption. It would be of interest to examine the development of products in the first category, especially those of which the

Table VIII

Percentages of Population Engaged in Agriculture
(Estimates)

Regions	1937	1950
World, excluding China and the U.S.S.R.	58	52
United States and Canada	23	14
Europe, excluding the U.S.S.R.	36	33
South America	62	59
Asia, excluding China	73	64
Africa	76	66

Source: United Nations Food and Agricultural Organization Production Yearbook, 1963, extracted from Table 4B.

Table IX

World Production of Major Agricultural Products
(in 1,000 tons)

Products	1948/1952	1964	Increase (%)
Cocoa beans	760	1,530	100
Coffee	2,240	3,160	41
Tea (excluding the U.S.S.R. and China)	545	870	60
Unshelled peanuts (excluding the U.S.S.R.)	9,600	16,700	74
Natural Rubber	1,550 (1948)	2,275	47

Source: United Nations Statistical Yearbook, 1965.

Third World is the sole, or almost sole, supplier. Table IX (p. 25) gives some data.

For the five products listed, the figures for world production are the same as those for the Third World, the sole supplier of all five products except for peanuts, of which the United States produces a modest 800,000 to 1 million tons. One sees that over a period of 15 years production growth ranges from 41 percent for coffee to 100 percent for cocoa. Even the lowest of these rates is vastly greater than that recorded for agricultural production in general in the Third World: 14 percent over seven years.

For rubber, the rate of growth is irregular and less, overall, than for three of the four other products; the latter face no competition but natural rubber has an industrial rival in the synthetic substance for which world production (excluding the USSR) rose from 570,000 tons in 1948 to 2,980,000 tons in 1964.

From this data it can be seen that agricultural production in the Third World is advancing at a swift pace as regards products destined for consumption or processing in the imperialist countries, and for which the Third World is the sole, or almost sole, supplier. Growth is less rapid when a product encounters competition from an industrial substitute (rubber). The main motive for production is certainly the demand of the imperialist market.

Considering the high growth rate for these products, a rate far higher than that seen earlier for Third World agricultural production as a whole, it can safely be inferred that the production of items in the second category (those for food consumption in the country of origin) is growing very slowly, or perhaps not at all.

Finally one can see that for the major basic agricultural products which imperialism needs, and can find only in the Third World, production is usually concentrated in a small number of countries. India, China, Nigeria, and Senegal produce among the four of them 65 percent of the world's peanuts; three countries — Ghana, Nigeria, and Brazil — supply 68 percent of the cocoa; Latin America produces three quarters of the world's coffee (Brazil alone produces almost one half); India and Ceylon produce 68 percent of the tea grown in the capitalist world; the three countries of Malaysia, Indonesia, and Thailand, produce 76 percent of the world's natural rubber. The mastery of the world's markets would be in a very few hands, if these hands would and could grasp it.

Conclusion

This study of the sectors of production can lead to some broad general conclusions: it has been shown that the extractive industries, which produce the major raw materials from the subsoil, are growing rapidly in the Third World, so much so that the gap between the production of the Third World and that of the imperialist countries is definitely narrowing. On the other hand the secondary industries, which produce the equipment and consumer goods so sorely needed in the Third World, are growing only at a modest rate, no faster in general than in the imperialist countries, and definitely more slowly if their production is related to population growth.

Development seems to be on the same order in the field of agriculture. There is rapid growth in basic products exported to meet the needs of people and factories in the imperialist countries; there is stagnation or regression in the production of food for local consumption.

To sum up, in a period of rapid political decolonization, the international division of labor which is the be-all and end-all of imperialism, far from being modified, has grown sharper: for some, the task of producing raw materials and basic products for export in a raw or semi-raw state and the sub-human living standards that go with it; for others, the factories, industrial expansion, and the concomitant high standard of living.

Chapter III

The Trade of the Third World

A study of the trade of the Third World and the imperialist countries, especially trade between the two groups, and an examination of its contents, geographical distribution, prices, and conditions all help to provide clues for a more exact evaluation of the real economic relations between them.

General State of Trade

In Table X (p. 29) I have tried to give a broad general picture of world trade in a fairly recent year: 1964. Since the exports of some become the imports of others it is enough to give an analysis of world exports, arranged by groups of nations, and by the origin and destination of the goods. This gives a panoramic view of the major channels of trade among (a) the advanced capital states, (b) the socialist countries, and (c) the Third World.

It should be noted that in this and later tables the values are given f.o.b., that is at the port of embarkation, whereas, when it comes to the values of imports, they will be given c.a.f., that is at the port of disembarkation. The difference between these two values for any one commodity is comprised mainly of freight and insurance costs. The first thing that strikes the eye in this table is that the exports of

Table X

World Exports by Groups of Countries and by Origin and Destination, 1964
(in millions of dollars f.o.b.)

	Total Exports	Exports to:					
		Advanced capitalist countries		Socialist countries		Third World	
		Total	Per cent	Total	Per cent	Total	Per cent
Advanced capitalist countries	116,015	85,539	73.5	4,462	4	26,014	22.5
U. S. and Canada	31,986	22,125	69	775	3	9,086	28
Western Europe	72,010	55,830	78	2,970	4	13,210	18
Japan	6,756	3,300	49	386	6	3,070	45
Australia, New Zealand and South Africa	5,263	4,284	82	331	6	648	12
Socialist countries	20,222	4,082	20	13,190	65	2,950	15
U.S.S.R. and European socialist countries	18,337	3,467	20	12,510	68	2,180	12
China and Asian socialist countries	1,885	435	23	680	36	770	41
Third world	34,725	25,617	74	2,175	6	6,933	20
Latin America	9,830	7,850	80	715	7	1,265	13
Africa	8,528	7,053	83	425	5	1,050	12
Middle East	7,546	5,480	73	400	5	1,666	22
South & East Asia	8,821	5,234	59	635	7	2,952	34
World	170,962	115,238	67	19,827	12	35,897	21

Source: United Nations Statistical Yearbook, 1965, Table 149. The presentation of this table in the Yearbook, grouping Australia, New Zealand and South Africa together, made it impossible for me to separate South Africa which is, therefore, treated here as one of the advanced capitalist countries although everywhere else it has been classed as a member of the Third World. South Africa's total exports for 1964 amounted to $1,456 million.

the advanced capitalist countries are over $116 billion,[1] 68 percent or about two thirds of the total of more than $170 billion. The socialist countries provide over $20 billion or 12 percent of the world's exports and the Third World almost $35 billion or 20 percent.

Turning to the question of which groups of countries receive the exports one is immediately struck by the following: the imperialist countries deal mainly with each other (73.5 percent of their total trade), the socialist countries likewise (65 percent of all their exports), but the countries of the Third World, on the other hand, deal with each other only to the tune of 20 percent of their exports while 74 percent of their export trade is directed to the imperialist countries.

In other words the first two groups depend on themselves for most of their trade but the third group depends on the imperialist countries for almost three quarters of its external trade.

The trade of the imperialist countries with the socialist world is very limited (4 percent of the total of the former) and Third World trade with the socialist world is little greater (6 percent of the Third World total). Since the socialist countries are outside the scope of this study, from now on they will be left out of this account in order to focus attention on the trade of the other two groups.

To get a better measure of this trade and assess what trends it entails, I present a variant of Table X (Table X-a, p. 31), placing the 1948 figures beside those for 1964 and covering only the exports of the non-socialist world.

This table enables one to draw the following conclusions:

(a) In 1964, trade between the Third World as a whole and the imperialist group exceeded $25 billion in each direction; but in 1964 the Third World showed a deficit of almost half a billion dollars, without taking import costs into account, whereas in 1948 the Third World had a small favorable balance.

(b) This trade amounts to 23 percent of the trade of the imperialist countries inside the capitalist sphere but 79 percent of the exports

---

[1] The term "billion" is used throughout this book in the American sense — i.e., 1 billion = 1,000 million.

Table X-a

**Exports Within the Non-Socialist World by Groups of Countries
and by Origin and Destination, 1964**

Advanced capitalist countries	Total exports (excluding those to socialist countries) in millions/dollars		Exports to the Third World			
			Millions of dollars		Per cent of total	
	1948	1964	1948	1964	1948	1964
United States & Canada	15,200	31,211	5,400	9,086	35	29
Western Europe	16,830	69,040	5,290	13,210	31.5	19
Japan	250	6,370	150	3,070	60	48
New Zealand, Australia and South Africa	2,580	4,932	475	648	18	13
Total	**34,860**	**111,553**	**11,315**	**26,014**	**32**	**23**

Third World	Total exports (excluding those to socialist countries) in millions/dollars		Exports to advanced capitalist countries			
			Millions of dollars		Per cent of total	
	1948	1964	1948	1964	1948	1964
Latin America	6,140	9,115	4,960	7,850	77	86
Africa	3,455	8,103	2,870	7,053	83	87
Middle East	1,995	7,146	1,300	5,480	65	77
South and East Asia	5,115	8,186	2,670	5,234	52	64
Total	**16,975**	**32,550**	**11,800**	**25,617**	**70**	**79**

of the Third World within that same sphere. In 1948 the corresponding figures were 32 percent and 70 percent. It can be seen that over a period of 17 years, there has been a significant drop in the relative amount sold to the Third World by the imperialist countries (minus 9 percent of their total exports) and, on the other hand, a clear increase in the relative share of the Third World's exports going to imperialist countries (plus 9 percent of the total). Thus it appears that the countries of the Third World are trading with each other less and less.

(c) These divergent trends are not produced by different tendencies in various regions giving variable balances. On the contrary, it is remarkable that the same trend shows up in the various regions within the imperialist group and the contrary trend appears constant for the regions within the Third World group. The changes noted earlier are, therefore, typical of the imperialist countries in general, on the one hand, and the Third World as a whole, on the other.

(d) In 1964 the exports of the imperialist countries to the non-socialist world reached a total more than three times that of 1948 ($111.5 billion against almost $35 billion). Over the same period the exports of the Third World rose to less than twice the 1948 total ($32.5 billion against almost $17 billion). This analysis lends support to the statement in *World Economic Survey, 1962*: "During the 50's the export volume of the less developed countries grew at an average rate of 3.6 percent per annum while that of the advanced private enterprise countries grew at almost double that rate, and that of the countries with planned economies rose almost three times as fast."

To sum up: between 1948 and 1964 the commercial growth of the imperialist countries was much greater in value than that of the Third World. The balance of trade between the two groups worsened for the Third World. The imperialist countries have come to depend less on the Third World for their exports and the latter has become more dependent on the countries of the capitalist group. In short, changes in the pattern of trade during this period served to strengthen objectively the imperialist character of the relations which subordinate the Third World to the advanced capitalist countries.

This rather gloomy picture might, however, be interpreted to suggest that, while the imperialist character of these relations is qualitatively more and more evident, there is a relative quantitative decline, at least as far as the industrialized capitalist countries are concerned, since they are tending to trade proportionately more with each other and less with the Third World. This might appear to conflict to some extent with what was said about extractive industries in the preceding chapter: that the Third World, although exploited by the imperialist countries, has a potential hold over them through its wealth in raw materials essential to them. This hold would obviously be valueless if its basis were found to be melting away.

We must not lose sight of the fact that, compared over time, the exports of the Third World to the imperialist countries continue to increase in value (from about $12 billion in 1948 to more than $25 billion in 1964), and that they are increasing even more in volume though not so fast as those of the imperialist countries (plus 50 percent in quantity from 1950/1952 to 1960/62 against plus 80 percent for the industrialized capitalist countries). Between 1948 and 1961 the indices of exports in quantities (base: 1958 = 100) rose from 62 to 129 for Africa, from 43 to 124 for the Middle East and from 53 to 122 for Asia (including Japan). It is only for Latin America that there was little growth (78 to 112). Statistics at current values sometimes give a distorted picture because they do not allow for changes in the unit value of the products which are far more favorable to the imperialist countries than to those of the Third World, as we will see later on in this chapter in the section on terms of trade.

In order to assess the relative strength of the imperialist countries and the Third World, one must also take into account the specific economic importance and prospects of certain export goods. This requires an examination of the composition of commercial exchanges between the two groups of countries.

Composition of Trade

Table XI (p. 34) shows the composition of foreign trade by groups of goods for the countries of the Third World (here described as countries exporting primary raw materials) and for the industrialized capitalist countries.

This table shows that the trade of the Third World is wildly out of balance: 85 percent of its exports consists of raw materials and another 5 percent of common metals, products of the first stage of smelting. Only 10 percent of the total consists of manufactured goods, most of which are textiles. Imports, on the other hand, are predominantly manufactured goods (60 percent of the total).

The trade of the capitalist countries, on the other hand, appears to be balanced and provides a rough model of the pattern toward

Table XI

**Exports and Imports by Groups of Countries and Groups of Products
in Percentages, 1960**

Groups of countries and type of product	Exports (per cent of total)		Imports (per cent of total)	
Countries exporting primary products*				
Foodstuffs	30	)	15	
Raw materials of agricultural and mineral origin	30	} 85	8	
Fuels	25	)	10	
Base Metals	5		7	
Manufactures, machinery, miscellaneous	10		60	
Total	100%		100%	
Industrialized capitalist countries *				
Foodstuffs	14.4	)	19	)
Raw materials of agricultural and mineral origin	13.6	} 31.9	18	} 46
Fuels	3.9	)	9	)
Base metals	10.5		8	
Manufactures, machinery, miscellaneous	57.6		46	
Total	100.0		100	

*The Third World plus Oceania.

**Some of the import figures for the industrialized countries apply to 1959, and some have been adjusted to give a total of 100, there having been obvious errors in Tabel 1—4 from which they were taken.

Source: U. N. World Economic Survey, 1962, various tables. The figures for 1964 are very similar; see U. N. Statistical Yearbook, 1965, Table 152.

which one would like to see the trade of the Third World develop. The category of fuel is affected by imports of oil, but for all other groups of goods the levels of exports and imports are not far apart. The predominance of manufactured goods among exports reflects the high degree of industrial development of these countries and the relatively high proportion of this same class of goods among imports shows that there is a lively, perhaps too lively, flow of manufactured goods among the developed countries that produce them.

The *World Economic Survey, 1962* is worth quoting in this connection as a reflection of the views of the experts at the United Nations:

> The reasons for the unfavorable trends in the external trade of the underdeveloped countries are rooted in the basic structure of this trade itself. Thus, primary products comprising foodstuffs, agricultural raw materials, ores and fuel account for well over four fifths of the total exports of the underdeveloped countries. For the industrially developed countries on the other hand, over two thirds of the foreign exchange earnings come from exports of manufactured goods. Only for the group of centrally planned economies are the exports of primary products roughly of the same order as those of manufactured goods. . . . The structure of the trade of the underdeveloped countries obliges them to export mainly primary products and import mainly manufactured goods. For no other group does the exchange of exports for imports rest on such an uneven keel; a good part of the international trade in other groups represents exchange of manufactured goods for manufactured goods.

Is all this mitigated, at least to some extent, by a trend showing that the Third World is beginning to catch up? Over the period 1955 to 1961 the annual rate of growth of exports of primary products was 5 percent for the advanced countries and 1.6 percent for the underdeveloped; that of manufactured goods was 8.2 percent for the former, 4.5 percent for the latter. The same United Nations document comments:

> Although exports of manufactures from the developing countries have been rising more rapidly than exports of primary commodities, . . . the rate of expansion has been about half that achieved by the developed countries. It will, therefore, be apparent that the developing countries are not even maintaining their share in international trade in manufactures, much less increasing it.

One might at least suppose that if the countries of the Third World are not increasing their exports of manufactured goods very rapidly, they are, after all, industrializing to meet their own needs first, and so reduce imports of manufactured goods. Between 1957 and 1961, however, such imports rose from $18.2 billion to $20 billion, and from 59 percent to 61 percent of their total foreign purchases. Thus industrialization to meet internal demand is still on a very small scale, as shown in the section on manufacturing industries in Chapter II.

For the imperialist world the Third World remains predominantly a privileged source of supply for certain essential products. In 1960 the Third World's share of world export trade (including the socialist countries) was: 36.4 percent of foodstuffs; 35.9 percent of agricultural raw materials and ores; 60.5 percent of fuels; 12.0 percent of metals. (Figures are from *World Economic Survey, 1962*, Table 3-3.)

However, neither the growth of the exports of the Third World in recent years, nor their future prospects, are uniform for the different groups of products or for the different products within a group. It should be observed that the prospects are usually good where the Third World is the sole, or major, supplier (coffee, cocoa, peanuts, bananas, citrus, sesame, fibers not used for clothing, bauxite, tin, tungsten, oil), but considerably less good for those products of the Third World which face competition from those of the imperialist world, be they natural or synthetic (fiber for clothing, rubber, copper, zinc, and lead ores). In the non-socialist world, receipts from exports of the main non-ferrous metals rose by about 40 percent between 1950-1952 and 1959-1961 but, over the same period, those of the Third World rose by only 25 percent.

This situation is almost entirely due to action by the United States and Canada which greatly increased their imports of bauxite but enormously decreased imports of lead and tin, and developed exports of copper and zinc; the total effect was to shift the United States and Canada from the position of net importers of non-ferrous metals in 1950-1952 (minus $344 million) to that of net exporters in 1959-1961 (plus $74 million). Over the same period, however, Western Europe and Japan increased their combined net imports of non-ferrous metals from $681 million to $1,331 million.

It would thus be unrealistic to pass a single value judgment on all the Third World's exports of primary products. It seems better to separate from the rest those products for which the Third World is the sole, or main source.

It would now be useful to look at the exports of some typical Third World countries, which will give a concrete foundation to this study. Table XII (below) shows the percentage of 1961 total exports which consisted of food and living animals, raw tobacco, raw materials, and raw petroleum. Taken together, these amount to all products exported in their raw state or after only simple primary processing.

Table XII

Raw Materials Exports of Some Third World Countries as Per Cent of Their Total Exports, 1961*

Country	Per cent	Predominate products
India	53	Tea
Federation of Malaysia	70	Rubber (over 50%)
Thailand	97	Rice, rubber
Iraq	100	Crude oil
Morocco	86	Phosphates, citrus and vegetables, ores
Congo-Leopoldville	88 (1959)	Ores, coffee, cotton, rubber
Angola	97	Coffee, diamonds, sisal
Ghana	99	Cocoa (65%)
Argentina	87	Animal products, wool
Brazil	94	Coffee (56%)
Chile	99	Copper (65%), iron ore, saltpeter
Colombia	95	Coffee (71%), crude oil

*Figures in parentheses in last column indicate percentage of total exports accounted for by specific products.

Further light can be cast on the matter illustrated by the above data by an examination of Table XII-a (p. 38) which shows the extent to which the advanced capitalist countries drew their raw materials from the Third World.

Carlos Fuentes gives other examples of dependence due to monoculture on the part of various Latin American countries: in Bolivia tin provides 60 percent of exports; in Costa Rica bananas 60 percent;

Table XII-a

Percentage of Raw Materials Imports of the Advanced Capitalist Countries Supplied by the Third World in 1962

Coffee	98.0	Crude oil	92.7
Sugar	77.7	Phosphates	64.5
Cocoa	85.3		
Tea	94.3		
Peanuts	92.7	Iron	49.1
Copra	99.3	Manganese	74.1
		Copper	57.8
Cotton	61.0	Tin	85.5
Rubber	75.5	Zinc	45.9
Raw timber	49.3	Lead	42.7
Jute	97.5	Bauxite	86.8

Source: United Nations World Economic Survey, 1963, Part 1, Table 5-3.

Table XII-b

Percentage of Total Exports of Some Advanced Capitalist Countries Consisting of Factory Goods, 1961

Country	Per cent
United States	67
United Kingdom	88
West Germany	91
France	76
Italy	80

coffee in Haiti 63 percent; oil in Venezuela 95 percent; coffee in Nicaragua 51 percent; and in the Dominican Republic sugar provides 60 percent of exports.[2]

On the other hand, it might be equally instructive to examine the data for a number of separate advanced capitalist countries and determine the part played in their exports by refined oil, chemical products, manufactured goods, transport supplies, in short everything that comes out of their factories. (See Table XII-b, p. 38.)

Some will be surprised to find the exports of the United States less typically those of a highly industrialized country than those of the other four countries mentioned. This is because the United States also produces agricultural and other raw materials on a scale so large that it leaves her with considerable exportable surpluses. The United States is the only one of the five countries listed which is a net exporter for the whole group of food products, raw materials, and raw petroleum (in 1961 $4,075 million of imports against $6,210 million of exports). Finally, turning again to Table XI (p. 34), the reader's attention is called to an aspect which is often overlooked: the relatively large imports of the countries of the Third World in foodstuffs (taking them all together, 15 percent of the imports of these countries). The proportion is 12 percent (cereals and their derivatives) for India, almost 30 percent for the Federation of Malaysia, 22 percent (sugar, tea, milk products) for Morocco, more than 14 percent for Congo-Leopoldville, 21 percent for Ghana, 13 percent for Brazil, 12 percent for Chile. The fact that a large part of the population of the Third World lives in a so-called subsistence economy should not mislead anyone. Imperialism has shaped the pattern of production in these countries for the satisfaction of its own needs and without regard for the inhabitants' need for a quantitatively sufficient and qualitatively balanced diet. The most basic food production is often much neglected, or even omitted entirely, and the climate is not the sole explanation. Was it necessary to wait till the end of the 1950's and the coming of independence to discover that Morocco could produce sugar, which it consumes to the tune of 350,000 tons

---

[2] *Whither Latin America?*, p. 12.

per annum? Or to appreciate that its dairy production could be increased to meet its own needs in that field?

Geographical Aspects of Trade

Table X (p. 29) showed that, in 1964, 28 percent of the exports of the United States and Canada, 18 percent of those of Western Europe, and 45 percent of Japan's went to the Third World. On the other hand, the imperialist countries received 80 percent of Latin American exports, 83 percent of those of Africa, 73 percent of those of the Middle East, and 59 percent of Southeast Asia's. Now, it would be instructive to look at the channels of trade of the principal countries of the imperialist group on the one hand, and a certain number of Third World nations on the other, and to try to lay bare the underlying trends.

In 1948, 65 percent of United States imports from the Third World came from Latin America, 29 percent from Asia and the Middle East, and the rest — that is, very little — from Africa. But, by 1964, the share of Asia and the Middle East was 30.5 percent, that of Latin America had fallen to 56 percent, and that of Africa had risen to 13.5 percent. In 1948, 59 percent of United States exports to the Third World went to Latin America, 27 percent to Asia and the Middle East, and the rest to Africa. By 1964, the Latin American share had fallen to 43 percent, that of Asia and the Middle East had risen to 43 percent, and that of Africa remained unchanged. Latin America continues to hold the lion's share of United States trade with the Third World, in both directions, but that share has fallen significantly over 17 years in favor of Africa in the one field and of Asia in the other. There was a noticeable tendency towards the geographical diversification of trade.

In 1948, 30 percent of British imports from the Third World came from Latin America, 37 percent from Asia and the Middle East, and 33 percent from Africa. By 1964 these shares had changed to 16 percent, 48 percent and 36 percent, respectively. For British exports to the Third World the shares of the continents changed from 1948 to 1964, from 16 percent to 11 percent for Latin America, from 45 percent to 48 percent for Asia and the Middle East, and from 38 percent to 41 percent for Africa. Here the major trading partner (Asia and the Middle East) not only remained the same, but actually increased its share in both directions. British trade with Africa also grew but that with Latin America fell considerably. Thus the tendency of United States foreign trade with the Third World toward greater geographical diversification does not reappear in British trade with the area, at least not by continents. However, if one considers changes in British trade with the sterling area, which is for her the most significant, one finds that imports from this zone fell from 36 percent to 32 percent between 1948 and 1964, and exports to it from 48 percent to 36 percent. The special links between the countries of the sterling area and its central nation were not effective enough to prevent a decline in trade between these countries and Britain, and in the case of her exports a serious one.

Imports of the six countries of the European Common Market coming from the Third World were divided as follows, as a percentage of their total: from Latin America 30 percent in 1948 and 24 percent in 1964; from Asia and the Middle East 29 percent and 36 percent; and from Africa 41 percent and 40 percent. Between 1948 and 1964 the exports of the Six remained at 22 percent for Latin America, moved from 28 percent to 36 percent for Asia and the Middle East, and from 50 percent to 42 percent for Africa. Africa thus remained the most favored continent in the trade of these countries, which follows from the fact that France especially, but also Belgium and Italy, formerly had major colonies and dependencies on that continent. There was, however, a considerable decline in the exports of the Six to Africa over 17 years (minus 8 percent), while, over the same period, their exports to Latin America remained stable and those to Asia increased. In imports, on the other hand, Africa remained stable, Asia and the Middle East made gains while Latin America seems to be losing ground.

This examination of the patterns of trade between the United States, Britain, and the Six of the Common Market on the one hand, and the Third World on the other, shows: (a) that the imperialist countries trade more with their former colonies with which special relations continue to exist than they do with other underdeveloped countries; (b) that a trend towards greater diversification of trade between the imperialist countries and the Third World can, however, be discerned.

An examination of the trade patterns of some Third World countries will show this tendency even more clearly:

The Ivory Coast took 62 to 64 percent of its imports from France in 1964 as it had done in 1958 but exports to the former colonial master country fell from 60 percent in 1958 to 36 percent in 1964.

Between 1958 and 1964 the French share of Morocco's total imports fell from 45 percent to 39 percent, while exports to France fell from 50 percent to 42 percent of the Moroccan total.

On May 5, 1964, *Le Monde* reported on French trade with Africa, of which half is with North Africa and a little more than a third is with the "associate" members of the European Economic Community, 14 out of 18 of the latter belonging to the franc zone. From 1960 to 1963 there was a decline from 22.8 percent to 19.3 percent of all French imports and from 30 percent to 20 percent of her exports. This decline can be partly, but not entirely, explained by the fall in French trade with Algeria. "On the other hand," *Le Monde* reported, "France's five European partners have trade relations with the associate countries which comprise two thirds of their imports from Africa and three quarters of their exports to that continent. This trade is growing steadily." If the application of the convention associating the 18 African countries with the European Six goes smoothly there is no doubt that it will accelerate the dilution of trade between the Six on the one hand and the Eighteen on the other.

A recent report of the Monetary Committee of the Franc Zone (see *Le Monde,* December 31, 1964) indicates that between 1957 and 1963, the share of the Six (excluding France) in the trade of the African states and Madagascar moved from 5.9 percent to 10.1 percent for imports and from 10.5 percent to 20.4 percent for exports.

Ghana, an African country not associated with the Europeon Common Market, took 43 percent of its imports from Britain in 1958 but only 27 percent in 1964. Over the same period its exports to Britain fell from 29 percent to 15 percent.

Turning to Latin America's trade with her principal partner: between 1958 and 1964, the United States share of imports fell from 57 percent to 53 percent for Venezuela, from 36 percent to 34 percent for Brazil, from 51 percent to 36 percent for Chile, and from 60 percent to 47 percent for Colombia. The proportion of exports going to the United States fell from 42 percent to 34 percent for Venezuela, from 43 percent to 33 percent for Brazil, from 40 percent to 34 percent for Chile, and from 69 to 52 percent for Colombia.

Table X (p. 29) shows that the underdeveloped countries of South and East Asia as a whole, trade less with the advanced capitalist countries than do other regions of the Third World (about 20 percent less of their total export trade goes to the advanced capitalist countries). Although not yet adequate, the diversification of trade is more advanced in this than in any other underdeveloped region, and these countries trade with each other more and more. Moreover, Japan, itself a member of the industrialized capitalist group, is a more important trading partner for the Asian countries than the Western imperialist countries.

This makes it the more interesting to analyze the changes in the trading patterns of India, the largest of these countries, and still a member of the Commonwealth and the sterling bloc. In seven years, the British share in India's imports fell from 19 percent to 13 percent, and that of its exports from 29 percent to 20 percent. Over the same period the United States share of India's exports rose only from 16 percent to 18 percent, but leapt from 18 to 27 percent of its imports.

One could lengthen the list indefinitely and find but few exceptions, such as Senegal, whose trade with France remained stable between 1958 and 1964. However, these examples of individual countries confirm the more general information presented and lead to two observations on trade between the imperialist countries and those of the Third World:

(a) For the vast majority of Third World countries the range of products exported is as narrow as possible; one, or two, or three products often providing three quarters, or even more, of the trade of a country. The number of countries selling and buying is also very restricted; a single imperialist country usually occupies such a dominant position that it can exercise every kind of pressure. This is almost always the former colonial master country with which the Third World nation continues to have special links: membership in the same monetary zone, preferential tariffs or prices, together with the advantages which spring from well-worn channels of trade. In the case of Latin America this privileged partner is the United States which is seeking to consolidate its present-day preponderance through the "Alliance for Progress" and the "Organization of American States." The major imperialists still maintain highly privileged positions in the trade of certain independent countries which were in the past subordinate to them. Such relations are facilitated by the disequilibrium of strength between the imperialist countries and those of the Third World; by blackmail to preserve preferences, exceptions, and special links of all kinds; and also by the lack of a solid common front among the countries or groups of countries of the Third World.

(b) One can, however, discern a modest, but generally present, trend towards greater diversification of the trade between the imperialist countries and the countries of the Third World as a whole. As the figures which show this have always been given in percentages, they seem to be beyond question. There is really a genuine, though as yet undramatic, movement towards the multilateralization of the trade between the dominant imperialist countries and the subordinate underdeveloped countries. The bilateral links created by colonialism are still strong, are often still the prime factor, but they are, nevertheless, beginning to weaken and give way to more complex patterns through which imperialist exploitation, as I believe I have clearly demonstrated, not only preserves its essential character unchanged, but is actually increasing the burden it imposes on the Third World.

Problems and Terms of Trade in Primary Products

It has been seen that the exports of the Third World grew less in volume than those of the industrialized capitalist countries in the period from 1950-1952 to 1960-1962 (plus 50 percent against plus 80 percent). The difference between the growth rates was even greater when measured in current dollar values: in 1964 the exports of the Third World were less than twice those of 1948 while those of the imperialist countries had more than trebled over the same period. The difference between the growth rates of exports by volume and by value can only be due to price changes which have been to the advantage of the exports of the industrialized countries as against those of the underdeveloped countries. Table XIII (p. 46), show-ing variations in the indices of value, quantity, and unit value of goods traded, gives an idea of this (the groups of countries on which it is based correspond to those established for this study).

The figures in the first two columns of Table XIII merely con-firm those already presented (the difference in the quantities is due to a slightly different period being covered), and special attention is drawn to the data on unit values of products exchanged. In 1962 the imperialist countries paid 108 monetary units for a ton of imports against 100 in 1950; they received 119 monetary units in 1962 against 100 in 1950 for every ton of exports: they were the gainers.

On the other hand, the countries of the Third World which paid 108 monetary units for a ton of imports in 1962 against 100 in 1950, received only 96 monetary units in 1962 against 100 in 1950 for every ton of exports: they were the losers.

This depreciation of exports and increasing cost of imports is expressed as a "worsening of the terms of trade," which is defined by the United Nations experts as follows: "the relation between the unit value of exports and the unit value of imports."

Table XIII shows that the unit value of imports moved in the same direction for the industrialized and for the underdeveloped countries, but that the unit value of exports rose by 19 percent for the former and fell by 4 percent for the latter. During the period under consideration the prices of manufactured goods, the principal exports of the imperialist countries, rose considerably while there was a decline in those of the primary products which provide nine tenths of the exports of the Third World.

Table XIII

Indices of Exports and Imports of Countries with Market Economies, 1962
(1950 = 100)

	Value	Quantity	Unit Value
Exports			
Industrial countries with market economies	251	212	119
Developing countries with market economies	150	157	96
Imports			
Industrial countries with market economies	240	221	108
Developing countries with market economies	179	167	108

Source: United Nations World Economic Survey, 1963, extracted from Table 1-2.

Table XIII-a

Unit Export Values for Countries Exporting Primary Products, 1959—1961

(1950—1952 = 100)

Fruit	95
Cocoa, coffee, tea	79
Fats and oils	87
Fibers	63
Natural and synthetic rubber	82
Fuels	103
Non-ferrous metals	94

Although this fall in price was general it was not uniformly distributed among the various categories of products. Unit export values in 1959-1961 stood at the figures shown in Table XIII-a (p. 46) for "countries exporting primary products" (our Third World plus Australia and New Zealand).

Only fuels (mainly oil) showed a slight rise but, according to the *World Economic Survey, 1962,* some of the gains shown for oil were of the "once for all" variety and "the rate of growth might easily slow down."

The situation described caused a deterioration in the balance of trade for almost all groups of countries in the Third World. This was due to an increase in the overall cost of imports concurrent with a decline in overall receipts from exports (see Table XIV, below).

Table XIV

Developing Countries with Market Economies
Balance of Trade, 1950—1962

	Terms of trade 1962 (1950 = 100)	Trade balance in percentage of exports		
		1950	1955	1962
All underdeveloped countries	88	plus 10	minus 3	minus 8
Latin American Republics	79	plus 17	plus 6	plus 4
Africa	90	minus 13	minus 21	minus 12
Far East	92	plus 13	minus 7	minus 35
Western Asia	95	plus 22	plus 26	plus 29

Source: U. N. World Economic Survey, 1963, extracted from Table 1–4.

Only the countries of Western Asia experienced an improvement in their trade balances, due to a growing volume of oil exports together with an improvement in the price of that commodity. For the countries of East Asia, on the other hand, the deterioration in their balances of trade became disastrously swift.

The decline in the income earned by the Third World countries from exports leads to a dangerous curtailment of their ability to meet the essential import needs of their own development. United Nations experts have calculated that "if the terms of trade for the underdeveloped countries had remained stable at the 1950 level, the total purchasing power of their exports in terms of imports in 1960 would have been $2.3 billion greater." They add that at the end of ten years between 1950 and 1960 the purchasing power of the major groups of primary products had fallen to below the average for 1924-1928. They recall that this purchasing power suffered losses from 1930 to 1940 which were more than recouped during the years from 1940 to 1950 and record that "in the years 1950-1960 a new decline set in and, although there has been some recovery in more recent years, it is not at all clear that the decline has come to an end."

The United Nations experts do not limit themselves to recording changes and making comparisons: they analyze the effects of these movements in a passage which is worth quoting verbatim in spite of its length:

Since exported primary commodities generally account for a large proportion of total production in the underdeveloped countries and contribute a significant proportion of the national income, instability on commodity markets has grave repercussions through their economies. Unless counterbalanced by government measures, fluctuations in export earnings lead to corresponding variations in domestic incomes, causing hardship to producers and distorting the pattern of consumption and investment. In the wake of falling export prices and export proceeds, national income tends to fall and, given the heavy dependence of most underdeveloped countries on customs duties as sources of revenue, government income also suffers. The impact on income and expenditure thus tends to be adverse for both the general public and government, and the result may be a reduction in both consumption and investment. In the face of a decline in the purchasing power of export proceeds, moreover, governments are often forced to cut back imports. When this involves a cut-back in the machinery and equipment and other strategic goods — the wherewithal of capital formation for which underdeveloped countries depend largely on imported supplies — plans for economic development are inevitably jeopardized. *(U.N. World Economic Survey, 1962)*

It is essential, however, to mention that the 1964 annual report of the International Monetary Fund states that in 1963 and the early months of 1964 there was a recovery in the prices of primary products, quite considerable for sugar and on the order of 5 percent for all other items (with the exception of crude petroleum, the price of which remained stable). This improved the terms of trade by about 3 percent for the primary producer countries (excluding those exporting oil). A General Agreement on Tariffs and Trade (GATT) report adds that this change led to a return to a favorable trade balance for the Third World. The International Monetary Fund report continues: "It is difficult to forecast how the situation will develop in the near future."

This data can be interpreted as an improvement from 88 to 91 or 92 in the terms of trade for the underdeveloped countries as a whole, on the basis of 1950 $=$ 100. Deterioration has slowed down but remains considerable and the change would not have affected our conclusions even if it had turned out to be rather greater than has been conjectured. In fact, the terms of trade for the underdeveloped countries were the same in 1964 as they had been in 1961: 97 on the basis of 1950 $=$ 100, after falling to 95 in 1962.

The problem of organizing markets for basic primary products, and stabilizing their prices, has long been receiving attention. The earliest international agreements were made in 1902 for sugar, in 1920 for tin, 1933 for wheat, 1934 for rubber, and in 1935 for tea. But all that is almost pre-history, for whatever had been done before the Second World War has been started again from scratch, under the aegis of the United Nations.

In 1954 the Economic and Social Council of the United Nations set up a Commission on International Commodity Trade (CICT) and meanwhile an Interim Coordinating Committee for International Commodity Arrangements "has been given the task of setting up study groups on primary products, formulating recommendations for the calling of United Nations conferences to negotiate agreements on these products, and coordinating the activities of these study groups and of committees administering the said agreements."

The General Agreement on Tariffs and Trade (GATT), the

International Monetary Fund (IMF), and the Food and Agriculture Organization of the United Nations (FAO) have taken further action, each in its own sphere, to deal with this problem. Innocent observers might jump to the conclusion that these problems must have been solved or be well on the way to a solution.

At present, international agreements are in force for only five products: wheat (from 1949); sugar (from 1953); tin (from 1956); olive oil (from 1956); coffee (from 1962).

These are only a few of the primary products which suffer from dangerously fluctuating prices with a general downward trend. In any case, the effectiveness of the existing agreements is doubtful. The agreement on olive oil proved inadequate to prevent a rapid fall in prices which continued from its inception in 1956 to 1961-1962 when some recovery was recorded. Since the international agreement on sugar has been in force it has not prevented fluctuation in the rate for raw sugar (covering a range of one to five). On August 12, 1964, *Maroc-Informations,* always well-informed on matters vital to the Third World, felt bound to describe the agreement as "not really operative." On October 12, 1964, the same paper reported: "In practice the international agreement on coffee has not produced the stabilization desired by both producers and consumers. The interests of the two sides are totally at variance and, according to market conditions, either the producers or the consumers have the advantage. At the present stage, the consumers are obviously in the ascendancy."

Although existing agreements have been so ineffectual, efforts continue to be made to reach new ones, with poor results. A proposed agreement on cocoa was the subject of a conference between producing and consuming countries in October, 1961. On October 26, 1963, *Le Monde* reported that this conference had broken up without reaching a successful conclusion and the paper thought that it was unlikely that any agreement on cocoa could be reached for a long time thereafter.

The World Trade Conference held in Geneva in May, June, and July of 1964, dealt with international problems related to primary products and many other matters of concern to the Third World. On

June 18, 1964, *Le Monde* reported: "On the subject of primary products the debates did not end in bringing together the partisans of opposing views." This vast conference planned institutions, and voted for no less than fourteen principles to prevail in the management of international economic relations. These principles were, however, the result of compromises, were passed with varied majorities (the United States opposed eight of them) and, finally, pleased no one. The 75 underdeveloped countries taking part issued a final statement in which they said that they "considered the progress made in all the major areas of economic policy to be quite inadequate to meet their essential needs." — *Le Monde,* June 17, 1964. Much ado about nothing.

Should the inadequate nature of the few agreements in force, and the failure of the 1964 World Trade Conference, lead to the conclusion that nothing can be done towards a solution of the Third World's problems of trade in primary products as long as the present political and economic division of the world continues? I would not maintain this categorically.

One thing to remember is that, while some primary products are entirely, or almost entirely, drawn from the Third World, others have their origins partly in underdeveloped and partly in industrialized countries. The voice of producers in the industrialized countries may be better able to make itself heard than that of the producers of the Third World countries.

It is, however, even more important to realize that the organization of markets and stabilization of prices for primary products might prove to serve the purposes of imperialist strategy. Success in this matter could well be the best way of inducing the countries of the Third World to continue for a long time to come in their role of purveyors of raw materials and exotic items for consumption (coffee, etc.), and thus to crystallize the present international division of labor which is one of the foundation-stones of imperialism. Most of the ruling persons, classes, and groups in the countries of the Third World are the objective allies of imperialism and, if the flow and the prices of primary products can be regulated, the following general line of argument might well appeal to such people: why go to too much trouble to try to process one's own raw materials now that their prices are, at last, stable and profitable, and markets steady and assured? It might be hoped thus to undermine one of the sources of revolutionary stirrings in the Third World, and to retard their growth and maturation. Similarly, it might be hoped that meeting one demand, which is important but not fundamental to the system of imperialist exploitation, would cut off, or at least temporarily slow down, the development of the basic demands of the anti-imperialist revolution. When hard-pressed, imperialism has, in the past, always known when to throw out just as much ballast as necessary, and when to give up some crumbs in order to keep the cake.

Does this mean that the anti-imperialist organizations and parties in the Third World should abandon demands concerning the marketing of primary products? Not at all. In any case, these countries can only hope to achieve the primary accumulation of capital necessary to get their economies off the ground on the basis of existing production, which is almost entirely in primary raw materials. But a solution which could be part of a strategy for imperialism, could only be a "momentary tactic" for countries of the Third World which were seriously embarked upon liberating themselves from the clutches of imperialism.

Conclusion

Trade between the Third World and the imperialist countries flows at an annual value of between $25 and $26 billion. This is less than a quarter of the total trade of the imperialist countries within the capitalist world, but it amounts to almost four fifths of the trade of the Third World countries with that same world. This gives a measure of the unequal strength of the two groups of countries in the field of trade.

The trade of the imperialist countries as a whole is growing faster than that of the Third World and, moreover, the imperialist countries are trading more and more among themselves and less and less with the Third World, while trade between Third World countries is decreasing and they are trading more and more with the capitalist countries. Their dependence on the latter is increasing.

Almost 90 percent of the exports of the Third World countries to the imperialist nations is made up of primary products and, for many of these countries, the greater part of such exports, or almost the whole of them, is made up of a very limited range of products (often of only one). On the other hand, most of the goods sent to the Third World by the imperialist countries are very diverse manufactured products. Not only are the countries of the Third World dependent on the imperialist countries for their trade, but they also often find their exports subject to the conditions prevailing in the markets for an extremely limited number of products.

Almost all the countries of the Third World have among the imperialist nations a privileged trading partner, which absorbs a high proportion of their trade, in many cases the greater part of it. The major partner, to which they are subordinate in trade matters, is the imperialist country which formerly conquered, "protected," or dominated them and with which they maintain special ties. However, these privileged trade links are showing signs of weakening, and trade between the Third World as a whole and the imperialist group of nations is becoming more and more multilateral.

Over a period of fifteen to twenty years the prices of many products have risen but those of almost all primary products have fallen. This has led to an improvement in the terms of trade for the imperialist countries, a deterioration in these terms for the countries of the Third World and, consequently, in their balance of trade positions. Fragmentary efforts to organize international markets and stabilize the prices of primary products have had only insignificant results so far.

I must repeat what I said at the end of the preceding chapter — imperialist exploitation of the countries of the Third World is growing more severe. A special point, however, seems to merit some attention: It has been shown that the foreign trade of the imperialist countries has been growing distinctly faster than that of the Third World, and more especially in trade among themselves, so that the

Third World's share in the trade of the imperialist nations has fallen considerably (from 32 percent in 1948 to 23 percent in 1964). Taking these figures by themselves, one might be tempted to conclude that the imperialist countries are "disengaging," to some extent at least, from the Third World. This would be grist to the mill of those who maintain that imperialism has changed its nature.

This matter must, however, be examined more closely. In the first place, the decrease occurred only in relative terms. Trade between the two groups expanded in value (from $12 billion in 1948 to between $25 and $26 billion in 1964), and even more in volume. Secondly, we must assess the degree of economic need for the trade. It is true that trade among industrialized capitalist countries grew rapidly, but what was the major component of this growth? As regards imports the increase was, surprisingly, almost entirely in manufactured goods. Taking 1957 as a base index of 100, by 1961 the imports of the European Economic Community stood at 110 for primary products but at 159 for manufactured articles.[3] Using the same base, the European Free Trade Association 1961 import index stood at 105.1 for primary products and 150.1 for manufactured goods. This trend has grown even stronger in more recent years. Paradoxically, those countries which specialize in making increasing quantities of ever more diverse industrial products, continuously import more of the type of product they themselves manufacture and export. It can be assumed that the goods exchanged are never exactly identical. Between 1954 and 1962 French imports of clothing were multiplied by five in tonnage and by ten in value and this clothing doubtless differed from her own products in the weave of the tweed or the Italian cut of the garments. Over the same period French imports of cars were multiplied by eight in tons and by eleven in value and these imported cars were differentiated from the French by their cigarette lighters or their trimmings. The economic importance of this kind of trade is almost nil and it is, moreover, multilaterally reciprocal. It would be of great interest to establish how much of the trade which has grown so rapidly among industrialized capitalist countries, is due to a culture

---

[3] *World Economic Survey, 1962,* Tables 4-16 and 4-19.

of advertising, snobbery, and waste, or at best is of doubtful or secondary economic significance.

On the other hand, trade between the Third World and the imperialist countries is concerned, on both sides, with fundamental needs. It is meaningful and correct to describe the products exported by the Third World as primary. It is not to satisfy whims that the imperialist countries import major food products and raw materials, but rather to meet the needs of their markets and factories for items which the former could ill dispense with and the latter not at all. On its part, the Third World buys the manufactured goods and machinery of the imperialist countries because it needs them desperately and does not produce them.

For lack of better indicators tons and dollars are used to measure changes in trade, but tons and dollars cannot measure real economic utility or the acuteness of the needs involved in the growth of trade or changes in its patterns. It would be more realistic to assign coefficients to the figures. In the meantime, though trade has grown more rapidly among imperialist nations than between them and the Third World, it would be an incorrect over-simplification to deduce from this that the imperialist countries are showing signs of "disengaging" from the Third World or that the latter is declining in economic importance.

Chapter IV

Imperialism and the Third World: Movements of Capital

Today's "pie in the sky" is "aid" to the underdeveloped countries. A great deal of material has been published on this subject, much of it full of factual errors, confusion, and mystification. The most serious authors — but not always the least dangerous — make learned calculations of the total production of the rich countries and that of the poor, of the differences in rates of population growth, and seek to determine how much must be withheld from the former in order to equalize per capita income in the two groups by the end of a given period. Some of them come to relatively optimistic laboratory conclusions — Q.E.D. — which tend to perpetuate the illusion that the problems of underdevelopment can be solved within the framework of the capitalist system. Imperialism is delighted to see these works proliferate, piles them up in its libraries, and returns to its business accounts. In all these analyses and design, even the most skeptical authors, such as M. Edouard Bonnefous [1] are in agreement on the principle of aid to the Third World. They simply want some other country to do more, and their own less.

For many, whether they write in good faith or not, aid is a kind

[1] *Les Milliards qui s'Envolent,* Paris, Fayard, 1963.

of alibi, a way of absolving oneself from the need to be aware of the exploitation of the Third World, and of acquiring a good conscience. Let us, however, cease to moralize, and pursue our task of measurement.

Evaluation of Aid to the Third World

Fantasy has run riot in the field of quantitative evaluation of various forms of aid to the underdeveloped countries. For this reason, we will continue to depend mainly on the United Nations documents bearing the title: "The International Flow of Long-term Capital and Official Donations," one of which applied to the period 1951-1959 and two others to 1959-1961 and 1960-1962, respectively. A further edition of this booklet covering the years 1961-1965 gives data on a different basis organized in a different way, so that it cannot be used for strict comparisons. The basic data have been brought together in Table XV (p. 58).

It will be noted that official donations and long-term public capital (loans) were much higher in 1962 than the average for the years 1951-1959. It was precisely during the 1950's that public aid to the underdeveloped countries was growing, and attention will be focused on 1962 — the most favorable year. On the other hand private investment was very little higher in 1962 than it had been on the average between 1951 and 1959. The explanation for this will be given later. The question of private capital investment will receive special attention below, but I feel that it should not be discussed under the heading of "aid," since private capital has never had any purpose beyond that of aiding its owners.

Since it is the object of this study to examine relations between the imperialist countries and the Third World these totals must be reduced by the amounts received from the socialist countries, which are given in Table 19 of the 1960-1962 edition of the U.N. booklet. The conclusion is that, in 1962, the aid flowing from the advanced capitalist countries was as follows:

Official donations: $2,747 million (less 18) = $2,729 million.
Long-term loans of public capital: $1,967 million (less 426) =

Table XV

**Movements of Long -Term Capital from the Developed Countries
to the Underdeveloped Countries**

(net receipts in millions of dollars)

		Totals 1951–1959	Annual average 1951–1959	1960	1962
(a)	**Official donations**	**11,737**	**1,304**	**2,384**	**2,747**
	Africa			889	1,121
	Latin America			236	278
	Southeast Asia			995	1,005
	Middle East			264	243
(b)	**Long-term public capital**	**6,728**	**748**	**1,747**	**1,967**
	Africa			541	629
	Latin America			256	204
	Southeast Asia			880	980
	Middle East			70	154
(c)	**Private investment**	**10,008**	**1,112**	**1,198**	**1,194**
	Africa			196	96
	Latin America			648	811
	Southeast Asia			252	173
	Middle East			102	114
	Total, a, b, c	28,473	3,164	5,329	5,908

Source: The International Flow of Long-Term Capital and Official Donations, 1951–1959 (Table 7);
1960–1962 (Table 11).

$1,541 million. Total: $4,270 million.

According to the 1959-1961 edition of the work quoted (Table 6), the net flow of public loans and official donations going from the developed countries as a whole to the underdeveloped, in 1960 and 1961, was respectively, 0.48 percent and 0.60 percent of the internal gross national product of the developed countries taken together, and 2.52 percent and 3.23 percent of their gross internal capital formation. By referring to the population table (Table I, p. 7) it can be calculated that the $4,300 million (in round numbers) of public aid to the countries of the Third World in 1962 works out at only $7 per head of population of the advanced countries (and $2 of this is repayable). This manna only raises the gross national product of the receiving countries by 1.5 percent and provides for their inhabitants only $3 per annum ($1 to be repaid). The flow will not bleed anybody white and there is no cause for wild enthusiasm.

What are the prospects that public aid will rise above the 1962 level in the future? The 1964 Geneva World Trade Conference voted in favor of a French resolution asking the industrialized countries to devote at least one percent of their national income to aid for the underdeveloped countries. Similarly, the United Nations set the goal that net capital supplied to the developing countries should rise to one percent of the combined gross national product of the advanced countries as a group.[2] However, the *World Economic Survey, 1962,* reports:

> During recent years rapid progress has been made in this direction and, by 1961, the net flow of capital [including private investment] from the advanced to the developing countries reached 0.7% of the gross national product of the economically advanced countries. However, the progress made in 1961 was exceptionally rapid and a slowing down is expected in the following years.

Even if no slowing down has occurred and the almost identical aims of the Geneva Trade Conference and the United Nations Assembly are achieved, the result will be a grand total of aid not more than double that for 1962 — that is, about $8.5 billion of public aid, or about $10 billion if one includes, wrongly in my opinion, private investment.

The Development Assistance Committee of the Organization for Economic Cooperation and Development (OECD) gives the following figures for 1965:

---

[2] United Nations General Assembly Resolution, 1711-XVI.

Public aid, $6,270 million; Private funds, $3,879 million; Total, $10,149 million.

This is 0.99 percent of the national income of the countries giving aid. These figures, especially those relating to private funds, have been stretched improperly and should be subjected to rigorous analysis.

The economists cited by M. Bonnefous in *Les Milliards que s'Envolent* estimate that to get off the ground and on the way out of their underdevelopment the countries of the Third World would require investment at an annual rate of $75 billion, while those quoted by M. Yves Lacoste in *Les Pays Sous-développés* suggest an initial rate of $50 or $60 billion per year rising progressively to $250 or even $300 billion. These estimates are rather lower than those of many experts who believe that a rate of investment of from 3 percent to 6 percent of national income is essential for a growth rate of 1 percent. However this may be, the targets set by the Geneva Trade Conference and the United Nations General Assembly stand at only one sixth or one seventh of the amounts which the most cautious writers consider necessary to enable the economies of the Third World countries to "take off"! It is not surprising that M. Lacoste considers it "very improbable that the industrialized powers will agree to make such an effort, at any rate under present circumstances," and M. Bonnefous concludes: "The needs of the underdeveloped world are so great that all forms of bilateral or multilateral aid will always be inadequate." The former writer thinks that one should look to the example of China and the latter counts on private investment by the industrialized world to get the underdeveloped world out of its backwardness.

So bilateral and multilateral public aid flowing from the imperialist countries to the Third World amounts to very little; its proclaimed targets are niggardly; there is a serious danger that they will not actually be reached; and aid on this scale is basically incapable of ensuring the "take-off" of the economies of the underdeveloped countries, or even of playing a major role in bringing it about. In fact, the 1966 report of the Development Assistance Committee of

OECD expresses the expectation that the growth of aid will slow down in the future.

Bilateral Public Aid

Bilateral public aid is more than ten times greater than the multilateral public aid dispensed through international agencies. Almost all official donations fall into this class as do almost three quarters of public loans. The United States is by far the biggest giver and lender but, in relative terms — that is, aid as a proportion of revenue or national product — France heads the list.

It is, however, far from easy to evaluate the real total of French aid to the Third World and the same is doubtless true for other "aiding" nations. In a series of articles in *Le Monde*,[3] Gilbert Mathieu attempted the task. He found different authors and different analyses estimating the annual rate of French aid at from 3 to 11 billion new francs. He himself tried to estimate the net, or real, level of French economic aid for 1963, that is, aid actually handed over, on the basis of the official Jeanneney report.[4] He reached an approximate figure of 5 billion francs, equal to 1.48 percent of the gross national product or, one might add, equal to the sum the French people spend on tobacco every year. But his 5 billion includes one billion of private investment, which I refuse to regard as real economic aid, and also 145 million of multilateral public aid. This leaves an estimate of 3.85 billion for French bilateral public aid in 1963, or 1.14 percent of the gross national product (1.2 percent if one includes multilateral aid).

No serious author today persists in denying that bilateral public aid, be it given by France or any other nation, has political conditions attached to it. A conservative French periodical published an article which stated:

This aid to the Third World is not gratuitous generosity, and it would be childish to deny the political, or commercial, motivations of what is

---

[3] May 10-11, October 22-23, 1964.
[4] A report prepared for the French government on its aid to underdeveloped countries and ways of improving it. This was produced by a committee of experts under the chairmanship of M. Jeanneney, who is now a minister.

variously called aid, technical assistance, or cooperation. It even happens that potential donors enter into secret competition to be the first to show their generosity to those newly admitted to national sovereignty. A glance at the map will show that nations without strategic importance get less than others.[5]

The United Nations *World Economic Survey, 1962,* recognizes that "the allocation of public money for aid is determined by political factors." Even M. Bonnefous goes so far as to say: "The first proposal that commends itself is to internationalize financial and economic aid to the underdeveloped countries and eliminate its present political character," thus making it clear that for him national aid has a political character though, in another context, he denies this to further his argument.

Bilateral aid is not disinterested, and it is often difficult to disentangle the intertwined aspects: the political reasons for giving the aid on the one hand, and the economic interests of the donor or lender on the other. In *Le Monde* (October 25-26, 1964), Philippe Decraene put these two aspects under one heading: "The search for prestige and the search for profit." He reports that: "In African capitals no secret is made of the fact that economic and financial aid is granted by Europe and North America partly to preserve certain areas as privileged sources of raw materials," adding that "aid does not necessarily fail to pay those who dispense it," and concluding most aptly: "This politicization of aid, and the concern felt to preserve certain economic privileges, go far to explain the incoherent and dispersed pattern of aid. The search for both prestige and profit prevents the drawing up of a healthy plan for aid to the underdeveloped countries."

Jean Lacouture's comments in *Le Monde* (October 24, 1964) are of interest though not always consistent. It is ironic to read the claim that: "Those of the former colonial powers which are really strong industrially have denounced the colonial relationship; they do not hinder, but even contribute to, the industrialization of their former colonies," and yet in the same article: "The best definition

---

[5] *Documents de la Revue des Deux Mondes,* November, 1962.

of neo-colonialism is perhaps as a situation in which rich countries invest in poor ones more for the benefit of the giver than of the recipient, and within the latter more for the benefit of the ruling groups than for that of the masses." The first of these remarks gives added weight to the second. M. Lacouture holds that "as long as French aid continues to be bilateral it will continue to be marred by neo-colonialism in the widest sense," and he defines French aid policy as one of "greatness indeed, but greatness requiring dependents." Criticizing those for whom cooperation means to sell at all costs, regardless of need, he concludes: "International cooperation is often a pseudonym for a two-fold exploitation: of French public funds for the benefit of private business; and of impoverished peoples for the benefit of local oligarchies." In this he is very acute and penetrates to the very heart of the matter.

In October, 1964, just before it was suppressed, the Moroccan Marxist periodical, *Al Moukafih,* analyzed new aid recently obtained from France. Pointing out that this aid could be broken down under three main headings — so-called "untied aid," "tied aid," and aid in the form of credit guarantees — *Al Moukafih* went on to comment:

It is only untied aid which really involves an injection of new money and this will be almost entirely devoted to the current budget which is known to be facing a huge deficit. Thus the loan will only serve to reduce the deficit in the Moroccan budget caused mainly by thoughtless luxury spending, and it will do nothing to improve the country's economic infrastructure. As for tied aid, it is known to be conditional upon the presentation of specific economic development projects which the lending country will then support by financing purchases, especially of heavy industrial products. Thus both tied aid and the closely similar credit guarantees are simply a means by which the lending country ensures a market for its own industrial machinery and equipment, by providing for delayed payment.

Adding that these three forms of aid were accompanied by a short-term loan of 6 billion francs, "an oxygen cylinder of doubtful value for a dying patient," the periodical concluded: "Really, France is using the unfortunate condition of our country to extract guarantees on the future of foreign monopolies and the indefinite continuation of the exploitation they impose."

It is also known that much of French aid to the North African countries is to be used for the compensation of French nationals, whose property has been nationalized or taken over. These few examples serve to show that French bilateral aid is, above all, a matter of self-interest; it helps to cover the luxury or prestige spending of the ruling groups of newly independent countries, keeping them respectful and attached to France; the part that does go to real investment is unplanned, and mainly designed to strengthen the position of business interests in the country giving aid, increase sales to the recipient, and to pursue and intensify neo-colonialist exploitation. It should be emphasized that the bilateral aid of other capitalist nations is a horse of the same color. All this kind of aid is both a smokescreen for imperialist exploitation and the guarantee of its consolidation. One can elaborate on Jean Lacouture's comment (quoted above, p. 63) to conclude that bilateral public aid is, in the interior of the country dispensing aid, an expression of class exploitation, since the tax-payers bear the cost while it serves the interests of business and the monopolies. In the receiving country it strengthens the economic and political power of the ruling class or group at the expense of any real improvement in the lot of the disinherited masses. When all is said and done, it is a means whereby the exploiting classes join hands across the oceans in international solidarity.

However, the data presented indicates that bilateral public aid is declining in relative value. Taking France again, as an example, public aid grew slightly from 1961 to 1962 but in 1963 fell to 100 million francs below the 1961 figure. During the summer of 1964, on the other hand, the United States Senate passed an amendment raising the rate of interest to be charged on development loans, and Senator Fulbright declared that this amendment would be a more effective cut than a direct reduction of credits, as was no doubt the intention of its promoters. In fact, total U. S. economic assistance loans, which had been running $1,300 million from 1962 to 1964, declined to $1,100 million in 1965, a reduction of $200 million.[6]

---

6 *Statistical Abstract of the United States, 1966*, Washington, D.C., U.S. Government Printing Office, p. 852.

On all sides, in all nations, voices are being raised to demand that multilateral public aid should replace the bilateral form. Some inside the imperialist countries take up this cry only in the hope that national contributions will, somehow, be lightened if they go through international agencies instead of directly from donor or lender to recipient. But more and more voices from the Third World are taking up the theme on the grounds that international aid would not impinge upon their freedom to the same extent as national aid.

It is this proposition that must now be examined.

International Public Aid

It has been seen that international aid is relatively small: constituting about 1 percent of gifts and 20 percent of public loans from the imperialist countries as a whole.

It is almost all dispensed from three sources: The International Bank for Reconstruction and Development (BIRD), more often referred to as the World Bank, the International Development Association (IDA), and the International Finance Corporation (IFC). Contributions on a much smaller scale come from the Inter-American Development Bank, The European Development Fund, the Common Market Countries, and from the African Development Bank.

This analysis will be limited to the major agencies: that is, to the World Bank and its two subsidiary agencies — the IDA and the IFC. To indicate the relative scope of their operations it is enough to look at the figures showing their net cumulative commitments up to June 30, 1966: World Bank, $6,299 million; IDA, $1,247 million; IFC, $84 million.

There is nothing "world-wide" about the bank but the name. Although it sprang from the loins of the United Nations and is associated with it as a specialized agency, the socialist countries, with the exception of Yugoslavia, do not belong to it,[7] nor do its operations extend to any socialist country but Yugoslavia, which might be considered a border-line case. So the World Bank is really the bank

---

[7] Poland, Czechoslovakia and Cuba were originally members but withdrew in 1950, 1954, and 1960, respectively.

of that part of the world which calls itself "free." It was founded in 1944 at the time of the Breton Woods Economic Conference and began work in June, 1946. Its function is to grant loans to the governments of member nations (103 on June 30th, 1966), to official bodies, and to private enterprises. It is a real bank which operates only partly on its capital and plays the dual role of lender and borrower, charges for its services, and shows profits. Over the last five years its long-term interest rate varied from 5 to 6.25 percent. On June 30, 1966, the profits for the financial year then ending amounted to $143 million (on a capital of $2,243 million, which means the rate of return was 6.4 percent) and its reserves had reached the total of $954 million (42 percent of the capital advanced). The capital advanced was itself only one tenth of the subscribed capital so that, all in all, one might say that the Bank is a healthy and prosperous business undertaking.

The International Development Association (IDA) affiliated to the Bank, was set up in September, 1960, and is organized on the same lines as the parent organization but operates in a slightly different and more generous fashion. It gives long-term credits (50 years with amortization beginning only after the first ten) which are free of interest. The IDA receives a yearly commission of only 0.75 percent on the accumulated total of amounts lent and not repaid. Consequently its net accumulated income, on June 30, 1966, after less than six years of operations, amounted to only $9.81 million for a total of capital advanced on subscription of $993 million.

The International Finance Corporation (IFC) was established in 1956, under the aegis of the World Bank, with the special purpose of encouraging the growth of private enterprise in the less developed territories. Its operations have been meager since its accumulated net commitments amount to $84 million, of which a little more than two thirds is in loans and the rest in direct investment.

The statutes of the World Bank require a majority decision on all matters handled by the Bank. More than 50 percent of the votes are controlled by six countries, namely, the United States, Britain, France, West Germany, Japan, and China (which, in United Nations language still means Formosa). The position is little different for the IDA and it is even better, if that is the way to put it, in the IFC where four countries (United States, Britain, France, and West Germany) constitute a majority. It is not hard to imagine the political preferences that influence the allocation of loans and the placing of investments.

The IFC report for 1963-1964 shows that body to have played a major role in launching some new developments and picks out as "especially interesting" the establishment of the new Nigerian Bank for Development and Industry resulting in "the creation of an institution in which the shares of Nigerian and international interests, private and public, are carefully balanced." Later in the report we learn that the Nigerian Bank is an extension of ICON, an investment company "almost entirely in the hands of British banks and industrial companies." The £2 million shares of the Nigerian Bank carrying voting rights are mainly divided as follows: IFC, 499,827 Nigerian pounds; Former ICON shareholders, 492,775 Nigerian pounds; New shareholders, 487,225 Nigerian pounds.

The last group is composed of foreign banks and finance companies with names that sound Anglo-Saxon, French, German, or Japanese. Thus, almost three quarters of the votes are held by capital of imperialist origin and by the IFC which is its mouthpiece. Indeed a "careful balance"!

Turning to World Bank and IDA credits, combined and accumulated to June 30, 1966, they benefited the various regions as indicated in Table XV-a (p. 68). It appears from this table that the Third World is not the sole beneficiary and that Europe received more than Africa.

An analysis of these loans and credits by the purposes to which they were to be applied comes from the same source and appears in Table XV-b (p. 68).

This distribution could certainly be criticized but one must admit that there is no trace of loans or subsidies to balance current budgets, and few headings covering small amounts that could be diverted to meet wasteful luxury spending, and no visible sign of strings attached

Table XV-a

World Bank and IDA Credits
(to June 30, 1966)

Region	Credit (in millions of dollars)
Africa	1,390
Asia and the Middle East	4,222
Australasia	520
Europe	2,147
Latin America	2,670
Total	**10,949**

Source: World Bank Annual Report, 1965—1966, p. 69.

Table XV-b

Purposes of World Bank and IDA Credits
(to June 30, 1966)

Purpose of Credit	Amount (in millions of dollars)
Electric power	3,368
Transport and telecommunications	3,945
Agriculture, forests, fisheries	1,004
Industry	1,726
Water distribution	116
Education	86
General development	207
Reconstruction loans	497
Total	**10,949**

Source: World Bank Annual Report, 1965—1966, p. 69.

to aid. Doubtless it is understood that Western experts, who work on the planning and execution of the projects, direct the external purchases required towards the countries they favor, and all is not pure in the distribution of the aid. As a whole, however, it does appear to be more disinterested and more usefully applied than is bilateral aid.

It is, however, not really less political, only at a different level. Bilateral aid is designed to support the policy and interests of France, or Great Britain, or the United States, in different places, and at different times. International aid, on the other hand, is designed to support the broad policy and interests of the imperialist camp in a more general way. There could be no better proof than this comment on the purpose of international aid, attributed to the late President Kennedy by M. Bonnefous in *Les Milliards que s'Envolent*:

> To help the underdeveloped countries of Asia, Africa, and Latin America to modernize themselves, and to safeguard their liberty and freedom of choice, at least for the future; to make possible the creation of new links between the Atlantic Community and the Third World, and to defend the frontiers of the free world everywhere.

M. Bonnefous sees this as "the real battle between communism and the free world." I knew this already, but it is pleasant to see it stated so crudely by an anti-communist: international aid is distributed by agencies which are institutions of imperialism cloaked in the garb of the United Nations; it is distributed solely within the bounds of the imperialist camp with the basic purpose of defending its frontiers.

The activities of the World Bank and its subsidiaries are on the increase, in number and in volume, while the reverse trend appears to be affecting bilateral public aid.

At the 1964 general meeting of the international financial bodies in Tokyo, 34 independent African states made suggestions to this end. In particular, they asked that the World Bank should relax its terms for the financing of projects and reduce interest rates; that the World Bank should seek to persuade the developed countries to increase their contribution to the IDA which, in turn, should agree to widen its field of operations; that, from now on, the Bank should transfer a

quota share of its annual revenue to the IDA beginning by immediately handing over $50 million of its $100 million profits for the
financial year 1963-1964. All the proposals can be seen to have the
object of strengthening the IDA, which is natural since its loans are
offered on the best terms. It seems as if these arguments will bear
some fruit but the most that can be expected is that it may bring
international agencies to the point of contributing enough to com-
pensate for the expected drop in bilateral aid.

Private Investments and Retransfers

Table XV (p. 58) shows that in 1962 private investment flowing from the imperialist countries to the Third World was little more
than it had been on average over the years 1951 to 1959 ($1100 —
$1200 million net per annum). From the annual report for 1964 of
the International Monetary Fund (Table 17 of the condensed French
version), it appears that the countries producing primary materials
(almost identical with the Third World as defined for this study)
received only $800 million in long-term private capital investment
in 1963 against more than $1,300 million in 1961 which was a
peak year.[8] Without paying too much attention to detailed figures, the
conclusion can be drawn that, over a dozen years, the flow of private
investment from the imperialist countries to the Third World has
remained fairly static.

On the other hand, as Table XVI (p. 71) shows, there has in
recent years been an increase in the flow of long-term private capital
from one developed capitalist country to another.

The IMF report for 1964 comments: "Judging by the preliminary
figures already available, the flow of long-term private capital to the
more industrialized countries has increased by some hundreds of
millions of dollars." It appears, then, that the trend shown between
1958 and 1960 continued in 1962-1963. This gives rise to the conclusion that private investment by the imperialist countries in the
Third World is not changing in terms of absolute value but is declining in relation to the world movement of long-term private capital.

---

[8] Annual report for 1963, Table 23.

Table XVI

Movements of Private Capital

	1958		1959		1960	
	Billions of dollars	Per cent	Billions of dollars	Per cent	Billions of dollars	Per cent
Gross total of out-payments by major industrial countries exporting and importing private capital	4.9	100	5.5	100	5.9	100
Gross total of receipts of countries which export private capital	1.0	20	1.7	30	2.0	34
Gross total of receipts of industrial countries which import private capital	2.3	46	2.6	47	2.7	47
Net flow of capital to the rest of the world	1.7	34	1.2	22	1.1	19

Source: The International Flow of Long-Term Capital and Official Donations, 1959–1961, p. 52.

The booklet, "International Flow of Long-Term Capital and Official Donations, 1959-1961" (pp. 52-53), comes to the same conclusion on the basis of the table reproduced as Table XVI. "The table shows clearly that a growing proportion of the capital exported by industrialized countries has been absorbed by other industrialized countries, especially the net exporters of private capital; at the same time the relative value of transactions with other countries declined." In another passage the following comment is added: "During recent years, long-term private capital has, in fact, shown a tendency to go to the industrialized countries rather than to the underdeveloped regions."

It is not surprising that this tendency is especially marked in the United States which is responsible for about half of all net, long-term exports of capital. The booklet quoted reports (p. 42) that, between 1951 and 1959, the amount of direct private investments flowing from the United States to the underdeveloped countries doubled but, over the same period, the amount flowing to the developed countries grew threefold. The same tune is heard from *Documents de la Revue des Deux Mondes* (November, 1962), which ends a study of the movements of American private capital abroad with the conclusion: "Such investment prefers industrialized countries like Canada or Western Europe." A later report in *Le Monde* (August 27, 1964) adds that in 1963 "American investment continued to be concentrated in Europe, where it grew by $1.5 billion (against $1.1 billion for the two preceding years)."

However, various measures have been taken by both national governments and international agencies, with a view to stimulating the flow of private capital to the countries of the Third World. *World Economic Survey, 1962* mentions among these: the system of guarantees set up by the American government, covering new investments against such non-commercial risks as war damage, expropriation, and inability to transfer revenue; a similar system in West Germany; preferential fiscal measures and international agreements concerning double taxation; attempts made in Britain and West Germany to set up special agencies to bring together private capital for investment in underdeveloped countries. There is also the project of the World Bank Convention in 1964 to set up a form of international arbitration to deal with disputes between private foreign investors and the governments of the countries receiving the investments. Will these measures have a marked effect? I do not think so. The guarantee systems set up in the United States and West Germany have had time to prove themselves and do not seem to have achieved very much.

Very recently, however, there has been some increase in private foreign investment in the underdeveloped countries. The 1965-1966 report of the World Bank sets the 1965 total at $1,350 million, to which must be added $840 million of profits reinvested, giving a total of $2,190 million. The report adds that this increase is largely due to increased American investment in certain countries which export oil (Libya, Nigeria), and in Latin America.

On the other hand, a study made by the American Department of Commerce [9] estimated that, in 1966, United States private invest-

9 Quoted from *Le Monde,* September 28, 1966.

ment would grow by 17 percent inside the United States and by 21 percent outside the U. S. (40 percent of the latter being invested inside the Common Market countries).

The flow of private investment from the imperialist countries to the Third World may be slow, but it is not without its rewards and compensations, for it is the object of capital to extract the surplus value of the countries in which it is invested with a strong tendency to repatriate this surplus value. Unfortunately, the figures which could be obtained combine in their totals the value of interest on loans and the value of dividends which, for the purpose of the present study, should have been displayed separately. Tables XVII and XVIII (p. 74) will help to appreciate the problem.

It can be seen from Table XVII that for all groups except "other regions," which include the less developed European countries, the percentage of retransfers has increased from the first to the second period in spite of the rise in the proceeds from exports. While the sharpest rise was that for the Middle East, the average rate of retransfers for all the countries considered is almost 12 percent of exports, a very high rate which must have serious economic consequences. The United Nations booklet which is the source for this table comments: "If this burden were to increase rapidly in relation to total currency receipts, there would be a danger that the countries would be obliged to change the quantity and composition of their imports. If such adjustments were to entail a reduction in imports of essential equipment, the rate of economic growth would be adversely affected."

Table XVIII is possibly even more significant. When net out-payments in interest and dividends are compared with incoming gifts and public loans as a percentage of total currency resources, the only region which receives more than it pays out is Southeast Asia. This region is a special case owing to the volume of public capital it received in 1959-1960, especially from the United States, for political reasons (see Table XV, p. 58).

The figures in these tables become even clearer when it is recalled that the Third World's net receipts of private capital in 1962

Table XVII

Net Interest and Dividends as a Percentage of Exports

Regions	Number of countries	1951-1955	1956-1959
Underdeveloped countries	49	9.4	11.6
Africa	8	9.9	11.0
Latin America	21	12.2	14.7
Southeast Asia	9	3.6	4.4
Middle East	8	13.1	16.8
Other regions	3	0.7	0.2

Source: The International Flow of Long-Term Capital and Official Donations, 1951-1959.

Table XVIII

Third World Income/Outpayments on Public Gifts and Loans as Percentage of Total Currency Resources, 1959—1960

	1959		1960	
	Net income from public gifts & loans	Net outpayments of interest and dividends	Net income from public gifts & loans	Net outpayments of interest and dividends
Africa	9.6	9.5	4.0	11.0
Latin America	10.8	15.2	13.9	15.6
Southeast Asia	22.5	3.8	26.1	4.8
Middle East	17.4	21.4	18.0	22.7

Source: The International Flow of Long-Term Capital and Official Donations, 1959—1961, Tables 10 and 11.

amounted to only one quarter of public loans and donations received in the same year. In addition it should be noted that the overall growth of public donations and loans has been slow since 1962, but on the other hand outgoing interest and dividends have probably increased sharply (new loans becoming due for repayment, new investments and reinvestments coming into production). This leads to the conclusion that, for the Third World as a whole, outpayments in interest and dividends must, by now, pretty well equal new receipts in the form of both public donations and loans and private investment. Even if, to be more than fair, one includes private investment under the heading of "aid," such aid can be doing little more than stopping the gaps it has created.

The largest of these holes is due to the transfer of dividends. Since the United Nations documents do not provide exact and general data on this subject, reference will repeatedly be made to the excellent work of Hamza Alavi.[10] He reports that, between 1950 and 1960, the United States recorded outgoings of public funds of $23 billion and receipts on public funds of $19 billion; over the same period, outgoing private investment of $20 billion brought in revenue of $25 billion. The author comments: "Total outgoings of capital from the metropolitan countries [in the form of private investment] are more than balanced by receipts coming in from profits made in the overseas countries." Carlos Fuentes has supplied further data: Between 1950 and 1955 the United States invested $2 billion in Latin America, and made there $3.5 billion in profits, of which $1.5 billion was returned to the United States. In the single year of 1959, the United States made $775 million dollars of profits in Latin America, reinvested only $200 million and repatriated $575 million.[11] Turning to the ex-Federation of Nyasaland and Rhodesia a United Nations report states: "Funds paid to foreign countries amount to a considerable percentage of net internal revenue: 10 percent to 15 percent. These funds are largely composed of interest and dividends, and of the royalties paid by the Northern Rhodesian mining companies. The high level of payments made abroad is due to the volume of foreign investment in the country."[12] The same work adds (p. 19): "The proportion of payments made abroad tends to increase when the price of copper is high. This is because the higher price brings about an increase in profits, and, therefore, in the dividends and royalties which compose

---

10 "Le Nouvel Impérialisme," *Les Temps Modernes,* August-September, 1964.

11 *Whither Latin America?,* p. 15.

12 "Structure and Development of the Economy of Some African Countries," 1958, p. 16.

the bulk of overseas payments." In other words, an increase in the value of a major item of national wealth is only of minor benefit to the nation to which it belongs. The World Bank report for 1965-1966 provides confirmation of the above. It estimates that in 1965 the underdeveloped countries had to find $3.5 billion for the servicing of their external public debt, and paid out $4 billion dollars in returns on private investment.

Nevertheless, there are many well-meaning people, both in the imperialist countries and the Third World, who still have illusions as to the usefulness of private investment in the underdeveloped countries.

It is simple to make the following calculation: a foreign private enterprise sets up in a Third World country where it makes a regular, yearly profit of 10 percent on its investment. If the whole of these profits are transferred abroad, at the end of the tenth year an amount equal to the original investment will have been exported. From the eleventh year onwards, the receiving country will be exporting currency which it has not received; in twenty years it will have exported twice as much, etc. If the rate of profit is 20 percent instead of 10 percent the outflow will begin twice as early. If only half the profits are exported the process will be only half as rapid. This example is a somewhat oversimplified hypothesis, but reflects reality. There is no end to the loss through such outflows, except nationalization or socialization of the enterprises.

Pierre Moussa gives a more complicated example:

Outpayments derived directly from the investment are greatest for enterprises in those branches of industry requiring a heavy capital outlay. Thus the great projects in Africa South of the Sahara . . . call for investments whose total is several times greater than the net output (from 2.5 to almost 7 times greater and usually 3 to 5 times greater). Suppose that a project is financed one third by capital and two thirds by loans at, say, 8 percent amortizable over 20 years; suppose that the capital is paid for at 15 percent; it can be calculated that outpayments on the loan and the capital over the first 20 years will exceed 10 percent of the investment; if the latter is 3, 4, or 5 times greater than the output, outpayments of financial origin alone will exceed 30 percent, 40 percent, or 50 percent of this output.

These facts give the underdeveloped countries the feeling of being defrauded, and the impression that their natural wealth is being exploited without leaving them much to show for it. In economic theory this situation is described by the term dualist, implying that the foreign enterprise within the underdeveloped country is like a modern oasis in the middle of a primitive desert.[13]

Unfortunately, this writer does not follow the argument through. He deviates into proposals for the traditional palliative measures, retreats to the point of suggesting that not too much attention should be paid to the dualist thesis, and points out that what revenue is left in the host country is a direct increment, which will engender new secondary and then tertiary revenue. I consider this to be a specious argument for there is no reason to suppose that these additional revenues will not, in their turn, be subject to deductions payable abroad.

It would be of great interest to know, even very broadly, what proportion of the profits made by foreign enterprises in the Third World is actually reinvested in the host countries. Accurate figures are not available except that the World Bank report for 1965-1966 estimates that in 1965 transferred profits from the underdeveloped countries amounted to $4 billion, and profits reinvested to $840 million. Is it, however, to be expected that detailed and accurate figures should exist? Figures dealing with trade and production can be regarded as firm data, beyond question except for small marginal errors in the groupings used, but one must exercise the greatest reserve when it comes to the profits on the undertakings and private investments of the imperialist countries in the Third World. In this field, official statistics and public service records, however technically correct, can only apply to the officially acknowledged portion of such profits, which often bears only a distant relation to the whole.

More and more Third World countries have drawn up and brought into force charters or codes for foreign investment. These set out to attract foreign investment by tax, customs, or other concessions, but purport only to reduce the amount of profit which can

---

[13] *Les Nations Prolétaires,* Paris, Presses Universitaires de France, 1960, pp. 46-50.

be transferred. Those foreign capitalists interested in investing in the Third World have understood very well how to take advantage of the benefits and are little worried by restrictions on the retransfer of profits. For those who know best how to extract all the benefits from the law when it is favorable, know best how to get around it when it is not.

M. Moussa himself recalls the well-known fact that much of the revenue of foreign enterprises in the Third World leaves the host country in the form of salaries paid to foreign technicians and specialists, and above all as payments for licenses and patents. Hamza Alavi adds to this list various commissions, administrative charges and other "services." But Alavi emphasizes the most essential point: "The greater part of surplus value is repatriated by the fact of the monopolistic prices of the goods sold."

Imperialist capital in the Third World is almost always invested in enterprises of one or the other of the following types: those which extract from the plantations or mines of the host country raw materials for the factories of the imperialist countries, or those which manufacture articles to be sold in the host country's markets but which are made in assembly plants from materials, parts, or ingredients which have been imported. As the concentration of finance capital and economic integration increase, more and more of the enterprises set up in the Third World are subsidiaries of foreign parent companies, or are dependent on powerful and complex imperialist groupings operating on a world scale. The first type of enterprise may find it very useful to export the raw material extracted from the host country, selling it at cost to the parent company, or another enterprise in the same group, which may be better placed to realize the potential profit. For the second type of undertaking to pay too highly for parts or materials to be incorporated into local products, gives the appearance of making less profit in the host country when that profit has really been made in advance by the parent firm or associated company from which the purchases were made. Groups with subsidiaries and multiple enterprises are thus equipped with a whole arsenal of devices for making their profits appear one place at one time, and elsewhere at another, as opportunities arise, but always with the ultimate object of making them available in some Western capital.

Profits made in the Third World and clandestinely transferred abroad by the capitalist companies operating there must be considered alongside those extracted from the Third World by great international commercial undertakings which scarcely appear there physically, but specialize in dealings in what used to be called "colonial produce," and is now described as "tropical produce." Carlos Fuentes states that Anderson Clayton's world traffic in Mexican cotton brings the firm five times as much per bale as is received by the grower.[14] A certain Third World country traditionally exports large quantities of secondary cereals and imports a great deal of sugar. Since it became independent, indigenous names have appeared on the customs documents. But these names are only the first, or rather last, link in the chain, and behind them there can always be seen the great international businesses which monopolize the trade in sugar or cereals.

And so it seems to be a vain undertaking, to make even a rough estimate of the total amount of the tribute which imperialism exacts from the Third World, or of the contribution such tribute makes to total capital accumulation. The few figures and proportions which it has been possible to give are only the visible part of the iceberg, and certainly much less than the whole. The most important thing to remember from what has been said is that, on the financial level, the presence of imperialist enterprises in the Third World eventually leads to an unending outflow of capital. The fundamental problem of the underdeveloped countries is one of primitive accumulation, to which the profits of foreign enterprises make a very small contribution, since the bulk of the profit extracted goes abroad, there to be transformed into capital which will strengthen imperialism, thereby making the relative position of the Third World in general even worse.

More can be gained by examining the nature and form of enterprise which is most attractive to imperialist capital seeking to invest in the underdeveloped countries. *Documents de la Revue des Deux*

---

14 *Whither Latin America?*, p. 15.

Mondes (November, 1962) says that "such investment is almost always directed to the sectors which contribute least to a balanced development of the economy," and gives as examples mines and oil wells. The IMF report for 1963 states: "Much of the foreign private capital investment in the underdeveloped countries takes the form of direct investment in primary production for export, especially in the oil industry." M. Moussa admits that "the search for raw materials is the prime motive" for such investment and adds: "The exploitation of the raw materials of the underdeveloped countries by the industrialized countries should not be regarded a priori as a crime."[15] I do not share this conclusion. "The International Flow of Long-term Capital and Official Donations, 1959-1961" examines the structure of capital exported by the United States between 1958 and 1961 for direct investment in the underdeveloped countries, notes that it is of the opposite type to that previously described for investments made in developed countries, and comments (p. 64):

The oil industry, extractive industries generally, and metallurgy made up more than half the total, while only a fifth went to manufacturing industry. In Latin America investment in manufacturing industry was relatively high, but elsewhere less than one tenth of United States investment went to this sector. The increase in American investment in manufacturing industry in Latin America is due to the fall in her investment in the oil industry over recent years. The smaller proportion of United States capital invested in the oil industry is not typical of the general pattern of United States investment in Latin America since the war. The oil industry absorbed two thirds, and the extractive industries almost one sixth, of all capital exported by the United States for direct investment in the underdeveloped countries outside the Western Hemisphere.

In very recent years, however, there has been an increase in foreign private investment in manufacturing industry in many Third World countries. In particular, there has been a proliferation of assembly plants (cars, tractors, radio receivers, etc.). Where an indigenous bourgeoisie exists, it frequently finds it prudent to turn from trade to industry, showing a preference for those sectors of industry which are technically relatively simple (foodstuffs, oleaginous products, textiles,

---

15 *Les Nations Prolétaires,* pp. 117, 193.

leather). Foreign investors, on the other hand, keep the control, or the initiative, in the sectors requiring more advanced techniques and forms of organization. The government of a Third World country has some power to direct indigenous capitalists to the essential sectors of the economy but is powerless, or very nearly so, with regard to foreign investors. If one such appears and declares that he wishes to set up a car assembly plant or a tire factory, and if he receives the answer that the plan gives these industries only third or fourth priority, he retorts that he, the investor, is a specialist in motor cars or tires, that he cannot invest in anything else, and it is a matter of "take it or leave it." He can only invest in this particular field because his purpose is to monopolize the market for cars or tires in the country concerned, and perhaps its neighbors. He knows very well that once he is established he will get the government to give him a monopoly or near-monopoly because his products will incorporate local work. For him, the conquest of a market is far more important than any concessions or preferences which might be offered to him for some other industry. The authorities in such countries are plagued by under-employment, and it is a matter of "take it or leave it," so they end up by accepting; at least a few hundreds, or thousands, of workers will be placed.

However little the value of such investment may be "for a balanced economic development," the first priorities of the plan will give way to the third and fourth because the former do not appeal to foreign private investors, often being industries that are less profitable or less directly geared to world markets.

Because of the overt or covert transfer of most of its profits, a private foreign enterprise in an underdeveloped country does not have an accelerator effect and plays little or no part in the cumulative process of that country's development. Moreover, it is rarely, if ever, integrated into the development plan of the host country and is generally a foreign "concession" within it.

Perhaps it is to meet this charge that more and more foreign private capital is associating itself with private capital, and sometimes with public capital, in the host country, and there are more and more mixed enterprises to be seen. Hamza Alavi quotes Daniel Spencer on India: "The chief reason for mixed investment is the need to circumvent Indian regulations for the control of imports" and confirms what has been said earlier in this chapter:

Many American manufacturing enterprises are less concerned with repatriating profits than with the sale of primary material (basis of the product manufactured) imported from the United States. The idea is not to extract the maximum of profit from the Indian subsidiary, but to enlarge to the maximum the market for the goods manufactured, so as to enable the American parent company to expand its production to the limit.

Mixed investment is the newest form of foreign investment in India. . . . In this case, the Indian interests are in a dominant position in relation to the foreign interests who control only a small part of the capital. This part is usually transferred in exchange for the privilege of supplying machinery and technical services. In fact, this type of arrangement can be considered as an extension of the technical assistance contract. The foreign company benefits from the contract which gives it the role of supplier of technical assistance and equipment and thus has an advantage over firms competing with it for new contracts.[16]

This analysis is similar to what might be said of mixed investment in many other countries such as, for example, Morocco. There, foreign capital is often associated with Moroccan private capital, or Moroccan public capital, or both together. The foreign capital is quite happy to be the minority partner, and even suggests that it should be, as evidence of the purity of its motives. It goes so far as to agree to a Moroccan Chairman of the Board of Directors, accepting for itself a deputy director or technical director, and why should it require more? It knows that the enterprise is viable only on the basis of foreign patents, foreign materials and supplies, and foreign technical capital. Although in the majority, the indigenous capital is the prisoner of its foreign partner. Mixed investment is, perhaps, the worst form of neo-imperialist exploitation for it ties up the indigenous capital of the host country and denationalizes it.

On the other side, one might mention the example of the industrial installations set up in the Third World by the socialist countries;

---

16 "Le Nouvel Impérialisme," *Les Temps Modernes,* August-September, 1964.

for instance, the sugar-refinery of Sidi-Slimane constructed in Morocco by Poland. In the first place the initiative came from the underdeveloped country which judiciously selected an industry which would utilize a local product (sugar beets), and operate to meet a priority need of the internal market. Is it because the firm building the factory was to be a builder and nothing else that a socialist country easily won the contract in international competition? However that may be, the winning Polish undertaking included in the project a level of local supplies which had never before been reached. It built the factory, trained Moroccan technicians and supervisory staff, left engineers in Morocco for as long as necessary, and then went home. The factory is to be paid for over several years, *in Moroccan produce;* it is the property of Moroccan public capital, and is run by Morocco for the sole benefit of the Moroccan economy. It no longer depends on the Polish builder for anything but replacements, a dependence which could hardly be avoided.

It is known, of course, that in other countries the cooperation and technical assistance of the socialist countries have not always been perfect. Nevertheless, in no case has their assistance constituted a "takeover"; it can be truly spoken of as "aid."

Conclusion

The data in this chapter provide the basis for an estimate of the public financial aid given by the capitalist countries to those of the Third World. In recent years this aid, including multilateral and bilateral aid, donations and loans, has amounted to about $5 or $6 billion per annum. There is little chance that this not very impressive total will be greatly increased, and even the most optimistic hypothesis does not offer any hope that such aid will be adequate to make a decisive contribution to the "takeoff" of the economies of the Third World countries.

Bilateral public aid, by far the most important, brings political servitude and economic subjection. It is given, received, and applied, in such a way as to strengthen business circles in the country giving it, and the local oligarchies in the country receiving it. International public aid is dispensed by international agencies dominated by the imperialist countries. It is technically better applied than bilateral aid but is, nevertheless, subordinate to one fundamental cause: anti-communism. There is at present a tendency for bilateral aid to decrease and multilateral aid to increase correspondingly.

For a long time the private investments of the imperialist countries in the Third World were static; recently they have increased in absolute value but much less rapidly than reciprocal private investment between imperialist countries. Private investment in the Third World is still directed mainly to enterprises producing energy (oil) and raw materials. A certain amount, however, is turning to manufacturing industry, alone or in enterprises of the "mixed" type. The industries are usually not those most needed by the host country, and are chosen according to the need for markets, often unbalancing the economies of the host countries. The imperialist private capital invested in the Third World sets up a great drain of surplus value, the greater part of which is legally or fraudulently repatriated to Western capitals, where it contributes to capitalist accumulation. This outflow of profits, together with interest and amortization of public loans, constitutes a heavy burden on the balance of payments of the Third World countries, removes the bulk of transferred profits from the cumulative process of development of the host country, in which foreign enterprises have, in all respects, the character of "concessions."

Chapter V

A Typical Neo-Imperialist Contract:
Association with the European Common Market

Having studied the reality of economic relations between the Third World and imperialism, it might be of interest to consider how imperialism conceives of these relations at the very zenith of decolonization, and how that concept is expressed in the institutions and contracts offered to the neo-independent countries. All the Six of the European Common Market, with the exception of Luxemburg, formerly controlled colonies so that the convention of association between them and eighteen African countries, signed at Yaoundé, in July 1963, can be considered as a test case.

It will be assumed that readers are familiar with the Charter of the European Economic Community (EEC), that is, the Treaty of Rome, and its terms will be referred to occasionally. However, it appears useful to recall the general, fundamental, objects of the Community.

Writing in *France-Observateur* (August 9, 1962), André Philip says: "The industrialized countries are, today, involved in a technical revolution which has made it impossible to progress economically or socially within the national framework." He continues: "The European Community was established with the object of breaking this vicious circle by creating a market big enough for the pursuit of effective policies to become possible in the future." The writer does not, however, disguise the political aspects of the Community. He desires the Europe of the Six to be enlarged by the entry of Great Britain because "the presence of Britain would anchor Europe securely to America and would make further attempts at neutralism impossible."

It is interesting to note that the Institute of Economy and the international reports of the Academy of Sciences in the USSR make a very similar analysis of the EEC, in their theses on imperialist integration in Western Europe, although, of course, writing from a different point of view and in different terminology:

> The integration of Western Europe (E.E.C.) is monopoly capital's attempt to reconcile the private capitalist form of the economy and the productive forces which have overflowed national boundaries. The authorities of the imperialist powers are seeking to transform integration into a Holy Alliance of reaction, for the struggle against socialism, against the working-class movement, against the national and democratic liberation movement, and for the strengthening of the economic base of the aggressive NATO block in Europe.[1]

Both assessments contain two basic ideas: The EEC is, on the one hand, an enterprise designed to increase the power of a group of already highly industrialized capitalist states, because technical progress makes it necessary to operate on a wider scale. On the other hand, this enterprise cannot be dissociated from Atlantic policy and NATO, being designed to strengthen it and make it more cohesive. Neither of these aspects should be lost sight of, especially when considering the relations between the EEC and the countries which were, until recently, directly dominated by imperialism.

The EEC never lost interest in the Third World. In the preamble to the Treaty of Rome the Six declared it their purpose "to confirm the solidarity which links Europe to the overseas countries" and to "ensure their development and their prosperity, according to the principles of the Charter of the United Nations." There is a whole program in the single word "confirm."

---

[1] Quoted from *l'Humanité,* September 18, 1962.

The Treaty itself automatically associates Algeria and the French Overseas Provinces on the one hand (Article 227-2), and on the other, "Non-European Territories and countries having special relations with Belgium and Holland" (Articles 131 — 136 and Convention of Application). Finally, in the Declaration of Intent annexed to the Treaty, the signatory nations affirm their readiness to propose to those independent countries which are members of their monetary zones, negotiations with a view to the conclusion of conventions of economic association.

The accession of a number of African states to independence after the Rome Treaty made the convention signed at Yaoundé in July, 1963 absolutely essential. It then became necessary to give contractual form to a system of association which had only been anticipated by the Treaty of Rome. This, then, is a very precise point of formal change from colonialism to neo-colonialism since, as we shall see, a year of negotiation did not prevent the new convention from embodying the essential elements of the old dominion.

It cannot be recalled too often that colonialism created the institutions which gave the "colonial pact" its full effect. The two major institutions of this kind are: the customs union or free trade area, as the case may be; the free movement of capital, usually combined with monetary integration.

The customs union or free trade area enabled the "metropolitan country" to receive duty-free from its colonies, the raw materials its industries needed, and the major tropical products required by its consumer market. Conversely, the markets of its colonies and dependencies were the protected preserves of its industries and the "trade goods" they produced.

The free movement of capital facilitated the establishment in the colonies of enterprises for the extraction of primary raw materials (especially minerals), commercial and banking houses, and the unlimited and unchecked repatriation of their high profits.

It is self-evident that the institutions created by a flourishing colonialism would not serve the contrary process: decolonization, that is, the attainment of economic independence for the struggle against underdevelopment through the autonomous exploitation of the wealth of the formerly colonial countries. One does not use the same implement for sowing as for reaping. The customs union and the free trade area effectively inhibit any real industrialization since, without protection, young industries cannot fight against powerful European industries which can, if need be, afford to "dump" their produce for as long as may be necessary. The free movement of capital legalizes the export of the profits made by existing and prospective companies established in the former colony, which is inconsistent with the accumulation of capital necessary for a rapid rate of growth. Moreover, the free movement of capital is incompatible with financial autonomy, in the absence of which independence can only be a façade.

It follows that these two typically colonialist basic institutions constitute criteria: any country or group of countries which maintains them in its relations with its former dependencies is neo-colonialist; any Third World country which accepts them over any period of time is accepting neo-colonialism, whether it knows it or not.

How does the Yaoundé Convention look in the light of this?

Free Trade

This convention between the EEC and the eighteen African states establishes not a customs union but a free trade area. There is no provision requiring the Eighteen to base their customs tariffs on the common external tariff of the Six (as is the case in the convention associating Greece, for example). On the other hand, the free trade area is of the classical type and the widest application:

(a) With regard to customs, the Six are to apply immediately to the produce of the Eighteen the tariff reductions which are to apply among themselves under the Rome Treaty, including past and future adjustments. When the convention comes into force all customs dues and taxes of similar effect will be abolished on the following products of the Eighteen: pineapples, coconuts; coffee if neither roasted nor decafeinized; tea packed in bulk; cloves, nutmegs, pepper, if neither crushed nor powdered; vanilla; cocoa in whole or broken beans. It should be noticed that all these privileged products are in the raw state, for the most part specifically excluding any processing or packaging for the retail market, and thus encouraging the associated countries to export them in the raw without themselves undertaking the processing.

On their side, the Eighteen must, within six months, make their tariffs identical for the produce of each of the Six. Moreover, the Eighteen are bound to progress towards the elimination of their customs duties and taxes of similar effect on all produce originating with the Six. (Reductions to be of at least 15 percent per annum and more if possible). This amounts to the progressive elimination of rights in favor of the Six, and no discrimination among the Six.

However, an escape clause, taken over from an earlier convention, provides that each Associated State can maintain or establish rights which may be necessary for its economic development or industrialization, or which would serve to maintain its budget. All the loud insistence that the EEC does not hinder African development, and is in no way neo-colonialist, was based on this safeguarding clause. However, protocol no. 1. annexed to the convention lays down that such rights as are in force on December 31, 1962, cannot be confirmed without being communicated to the Council of Association, and are subject to consultation if the EEC should so request. The same procedure would apply to any subsequent creation or increase of protective rights. Thus the continuation or creation of rights is subject to the consent of the Council of Association, a body which has equal representation of both sides and which can make pronouncements by *common accord* between the Community and the Associated States. It is perfectly possible that some rights of this nature will be asked for and agreed to: the Community would be very foolish if it did not make some concessions. It is clear, however, that such rights are a departure from the rule, and require a precisely laid down procedure to bring them into being. The common accord is equivalent to a right of veto for the Community. It follows that the Eighteen are not free to pursue their economic development, that they are under tutelage, and can only hope for a few exceptions to the rule which strangles them. Does not the convention itself "give the show away" in stating that rights necessary for the economic development of the African Associates can only be established by exemption? Is this not a confession that the norm (of the convention) hinders economic development and industrialization? If the exemptions were intended to apply more often than the rule then they would be the rule and the reverse situation the exemption.

(b) In the field of removing restrictive quotas, the convention provides that the Six will extend to the Eighteen the benefit of the elimination of quantitative restrictions as it is applied among themselves.

On their side, the Associated States are bound to eliminate all quantitative restrictions on the import of products originating from the Six, over a period of not more than four years. This process of elimination to be progressive and non-discriminatory (total quotas). As was the case for tariff reductions, provision is made for exemptions enabling the Eighteen to preserve or establish quantitative restrictions required to meet the needs of their economic development and industrialization, or if they encounter balance of payments difficulties, or with regard to agricultural products if these are subject to the provisions of existing regional marketing organizations. These exemptions, like the others, are subject to prior consultation within the Council of Association, and the comments previously made are equally applicable in this case.

(c) Some rather vague provisions relative to certain agricultural produce, and to trade policy, can be ignored, but attention must be drawn to a reciprocal and general escape clause which provides that some or all of the Six or the Eighteen may introduce the measures necessary to deal with any serious disturbance of a sector of their economies. Provision is made for consultation, the measures introduced must interfere with the operation of the Association as little as possible, and must not be more far-reaching than is absolutely essential to meet the difficulties concerned.

Reciprocity and Non-Discrimination

The new Convention of Association between the EEC and the eighteen African countries provides the greatest reciprocal freedom for the citizens and companies of the Six to set up business inside the Eighteen, and vice-versa, on the basis of the dual role of reciprocity and non-discrimination. The sense of equality cherished by every honest man will be comforted by the "vice-versa": if the business men and trusts of the Six are free to set up in the Associated States, the business men and trusts of the Eighteen are equally free to set up in the Six. Who would dare call this egalitarian provision neo-colonialist?

Most deserving of our attention, however, are the provisions for the free movement of capital. The Convention stipulates that the Eighteen will make every effort to avoid the introduction of any new exchange restriction affecting the control of investments and current payments related to the movement of capital, when these investments and payments are made by the citizens of the Six. It adds that the Eighteen undertake, at the latest by January 1, 1965, to treat the citizens and companies of the Six equally in matters concerning investments made by them after the entry into effect of the Convention, and the movements of capital to which such investments give rise.

Once more, the rule is non-discrimination among the Six on the part of the Eighteen. One cannot appreciate the importance of this rule without bearing in mind the fact that all the Eighteen belong to a monetary zone under the leadership of one or another of the Six. Fourteen belong to the zone of the French franc, three to that of the Belgian franc, and one to that of the lira. Within these zones movements of capital and transfers are free. Non-discrimination thus amounts to bringing five of the Six into line with the sixth which already enjoys a position of privilege with one or several of the Eighteen. In practice the free movement of capital becomes the rule among the Six and the Eighteen. The freedom to set up business is really co-extensive with freedom of payments and free movement of capital.

Conclusion

An old dream has come true, the words of the preamble have been justified ("to *confirm* the solidarity which links Europe with the overseas countries"). The bias in the Yaoundé convention has enabled the EEC to set up a real Eurafrican common market encompassing the Six and their eighteen African associates. Without restriction by quota or customs charges, goods will be exchanged within this vast area where the European and African economies complement each other. This is the traditional form of free trade area, to be modified only by a few exemptions. Business undertakings and capital will be exchanged as freely as goods; so much has been said earlier about the heavy drain which foreign private investment imposes on the countries of the Third World that there is no need to repeat it here.

This structure will result in the perpetuation of the imperialist type of international division of labor: for some countries primary production; for others, manufacturing industry. While it is true that Europe has no call to produce bananas, coffee, cocoa, or mahogany — the countries of Africa have as much call, and more than have many others, to make textiles, leather and leather goods, oils and vegetable fats, to process their own timber, and above all, to process their own ores and create the secondary industries based upon them. However, such industries, especially the heavy industries, will not develop because the Yaoundé Convention sets up a system which is essentially, typically, one of classical colonial exploitation. It differs from such a system only in three respects:

(a) It is multilateral. Instead of two partners, one European and one African, we now have six European, and eighteen African partners. It can be said that the EEC has turned colonialism into a co-operative enterprise or a joint stock company.

(b) Instead of being imposed by conquest, it has been set up by contractual agreement between the European states and the African Associates. This does not, however, change its nature: the fact that African governments have put their signatures to the convention has no magic power to change its character.

(c) It is wrapped in a fog of hypocrisy and paternalism. In 1963 neo-colonialism had to wear kid gloves which were not necessary to the old colonialism. As we have seen, it has been obliged to concede various exemptions and escape clauses, which may, however, do more harm than good. Their practical effect will be very limited; yet they camouflage reality from the superficial observer, and give an air of respectability to the Six and the Eighteen. The Convention is full of fine words which dress up the association as a rescue operation to help the Associated States with their development. But fairness must be preserved: the Convention does match the word with some provision for practical aid which deserves to be examined more closely.

In fact, one chapter of the Convention is devoted to financial and technical cooperation, for which purpose the EEC is to make available to the Eighteen a total sum of $730 million over five years. Of this sum $620 million is non-returnable and $110 million is to be repaid. Even being generous enough to lump it all together, this contribution is far less than the annual sum spent at their race-courses by the inhabitants of the Six; it will drain less than one dollar per head per year from "little Europe," and give a bonus of less than two and a half dollars a year to each African concerned. Another way of putting it is that it amounts to 3 percent of the accumulated internal gross national product of the Eighteen.

The latter will not, however, be free to season this modest dish to suit themselves. In fact, the Convention lays down that single states or groups of states shall submit to the ECC details of the projects for which they seek assistance. The EEC will assess the projects and the state or group of states making the request is then to be "informed of the result of its request." The word "tutelage" appeared above; it must be repeated here. This tutelage is not made less easy to bear by the fact that the Council of Association is to have the task of laying down the general pattern of financial and technical cooperation on the basis of annual reports. The nature of this "pattern" is vague and general, while, on the contrary, procedure laid down for the examination of projects is precisely defined and might be said to be "line by line."

Another point deserves mention here. Part of the aid contributed by the Six is reserved for the progressive adaptation of the prices of products of the Eighteen to world market rates. In fact, some colonialist countries agreed to buy certain of the products of their colonies at privileged prices, considerably higher than those current on the world market. In the period of bilateral colonialism this seemed a justifiable partial compensation but in the era of multinational neo-colonialism it has apparently lost its justification, for the Convention lays down timetables for the adaptation of the prices of various products or groups of products of the Eighteen to world market prices. This gives rise to the reflection that the Community itself will be the beneficiary of that portion of its aid contribution devoted to this purpose.

One of the most striking features of the Yaoundé Convention is its lack of originality; it is of the type called "open," that is to say that new African states can adhere to it. Even for those who wish to make an agreement with the Community without becoming full associates, the Convention is a clear point of reference. This was noted by André Pautard in an article in *Le Monde* (November 22-23, 1964) about the negotiations between the Six and the three North African countries. He says that the three countries of the Maghreb (Algeria, Tunisia, and Morocco) were afraid to commit themselves as deeply as the Eighteen and, therefore, envisaged some form of "modified free trade area," in which the poor countries would not have to sacrifice their customs as completely as the rich, and would not have to drop all the barriers protecting their local industries. They rejected an agreement which would imply some sort of integration as its end result, and were hesitant even about the term "association" because of the political commitment it seemed to imply.

Many of those in authority in the Third World prefer international public aid to bilateral aid, but it must be admitted that the European Common Market is very attractive to a number of African leaders who see in it the extension of formerly bilateral links to a group of countries, an opportunity to lighten the subjection which formerly weighed upon them. I believe this idea to be quite misconceived. It arises from a failure to understand the basic unity of imperialism, despite apparent contradictions within it.

In the days before the growth rate of the Six began to fall off, inflation raised its ugly head, hourly rates began to fall and social conflicts to appear, goods became hard to sell and "miracles began to fade": the attractions of the EEC, aided by voluminous exaggerated propaganda, gave rise to the curious proliferation of projects for common markets among the countries of the Third World: African common market, Arab common market, North African common market.

Such projects show an imitative spirit which has been eloquently condemned by Frantz Fanon. It is self-evident that if the Six made the Rome Treaty as it is and not otherwise, this was not in consideration of the special features of the economic situation in Senegal, the Cameroons, or Tunisia, but in direct relation to the economic situation of the Six themselves, not to mention the political and strategic needs mentioned at the beginning of this chapter. What is there in common between the national economies, the development of productive forces in the countries on the European and on the African sides of the Mediterranean? There is no need to recapitulate all that has been said about the countries of the Third World in general, in Chapters II and III especially; it all applies to Africa. One example will suffice: if one recognizes that an iron and steel industry is the basis of industrialization, one must see the significance of the fact that each of the European Six has such an industry, while no African country, with the sole exception of the Union of South Africa, has yet established one.

What would be the purpose of African common markets? It has been seen that the Third World as a whole trades but little within its own confines. Africa, which is the most backward part of it, has only a very small volume of trade inside the continent. This is one of the most direct effects of the present pattern, deliberately created by imperialism, upon the productive forces of Africa. As long as the present structures remain in existence, the creation of common markets, the removal of customs barriers and quotas, will serve little purpose, except in a small number of special cases which could easily be provided for by separate arrangements. In general, what African country will buy the timber, the coffee, the oil-seeds, the cocoa, or the bananas of another? What North African country would offer an outlet for the phosphates, the citrus, the early fruits and vegetables, the wines, of the others? At the present time where would the ores, the rubber, and the fibers of the African producers find factories to process them in other African countries? The patterns of production are the determinant factors: it is they that must be transformed before anything else can be achieved.

The Convention associating the eighteen African countries with the European Common Market appears to be an attempt to contractualize and institutionalize links between a group of imperialist countries and a number of Third World countries. It shows that imperialism has remained true to itself; its real face is unchanged, under the mask; the system which has been set up is only the old colonial pact, softened just sufficiently to mislead people. The financial aid of the Six is only the sugar-coating on the pill.

The major innovation of this convention is the change from bilateral to multilateral imperialist links. The operations of imperialism are tending to become denationalized.

Chapter VI

Conclusion

At the end of each chapter I briefly summarized the incomplete conclusions. They all tended to show that in the very peak period of political decolonization imperialist exploitation not only persists but is becoming harsher. The international division of labor characteristic of imperialism becomes more and more marked, the underdeveloped countries produce and export more and more primary products (foodstuffs, power, and raw materials), the industrialized capitalist countries produce and export more and more manufactured goods. The terms of trade continue to move against the former, the private capital of the latter invested in the Third World is still directed mainly to the development of petroleum and raw materials, and its purpose remains the direct or indirect extraction of the highest possible rate of profit. The supposedly original structures set up by imperialism (e.g. associate membership in the Common Market) serve to extend the life of the old colonial relationship while attempting to camouflage it. Only one new fact emerges: aid, or assistance. Imperialism, however, cannot but seek to distort this for its own benefit and the proportion which is, nevertheless, useful is too small to be effective. It is both a pittance and a mirage.

Nothing really new has happened. The sun of imperialism still glares down on the most impoverished half of the planet, rather more fiercely than before. It would be easy to leave it at that, but things are not so simple. A picture drawn in broad outline can be a good likeness and at the same time misleading: it must be examined in greater detail.

Almost half a century ago, when the First World War was at its height and the earliest signs of the October revolution were still invisible, Lenin produced his masterly analysis and definition of imperialism. It would be difficult to discuss present-day imperialism without reference to his work. I do not propose to go back on his analysis and definition but I do want to pay some attention to two aspects of the imperialism of the years 1910-1920 which were emphasized by Lenin but are no longer characteristic of imperialism in the 1950's and 1960's. There would be little value in repeating after Lenin (and less well than he expressed it) what has remained unchanged in the physiognomy of imperialism but it may, on the other hand, be instructive to study those aspects of it which have changed.

Lenin attributes particular importance to the export of capital, especially to underdeveloped countries, as characteristic of the imperialist stage of capitalism. "In these backward countries," he writes, "profits are usually high for capital is scarce, the price of land is relatively low, wages are low, raw materials are cheap. . . . The necessity for exporting capital arises from the fact that in a few countries capitalism has become 'over-ripe,' and, owing to the backward stage of agriculture and the impoverishment of the masses, capitalism lacks opportunities for 'profitable' investment." [1]

Hamza Alavi in *Le Nouvel Impérialisme* defines the Leninist analysis of this point well when he writes: "The key-stone of this theory is the problem of an outlet for excess capital which was then growing rapidly as a consequence of the disparity between expanding productive forces and limited consumption inherent in the capitalist system." The race of monopolistic capital to achieve a hegemony on the one hand, and the attraction of a higher rate of profit to be gained by colonial exploitation on the other, are two factors which accelerate

---

[1] *Imperialism, The Highest Stage of Capitalism,* Chapter IV.

the drive for expansion overseas of surplus capital accumulated in the advanced countries.

In Chapter IV it was noted that private investments flowing from the advanced countries to the Third World tend to stagnate or grow very slowly while the movement of private capital among the advanced countries themselves increases rapidly. This is contrary to the Leninist picture, which was undoubtedly accurate when it was drawn but does not seem to correspond with present-day reality. We do not claim to offer a complete explanation of this but only to present some of the elements of an explanation.

In the first place it is not certain that all enterprises in the Third World still yield a higher rate of profit than their equivalents in highly industrialized countries. Low wages, minimal land prices, etc., are not such good bets in the present period of very advanced industrial technology requiring an increasingly skilled labor force and giving rise to rapidly rising productivity in the advanced countries.

Secondly, political decolonization and the precarious tenure of most of the governments of the neo-independent countries give rise to what the IMF calls "lack of confidence" in the minds of major foreign investors. This expression recurs like a theme song in the publications of the IMF.

I have emphasized the fact that investments by the imperialist countries in the Third World mostly relate to petroleum and raw materials. Where such investment does go to secondary industry it is because this has become necessary to conquer or preserve a market. In such cases there is often an association with local public or private capital which has a number of advantages and provides some insurance against political risks.

Imperialist private capital knows that the Third World is a transitional phenomenon. Given the choice now between a copper mine in Katanga and one in Europe, Europe would come first whereas there is no doubt that in Lenin's day it would have been Katanga; but minerals and petroleum do not offer this choice and must be extracted where deposits are found. On the other hand, imperialist private capital does have such a choice where secondary industry is concerned and there is no doubt that investment at home is usually preferred.

Here one finds oneself in agreement with Hamza Alavi who sees neo-colonialism or the new imperialism as "seeking rather to concentrate investment in the metropolitan countries so as to develop national production, dominate the world market and strengthen its hold on it in every possible way." He also states: "The tendency to export capital is only one reflection of monopoly capitalism and its drive to dominate all sources of raw materials and market opportunities."

It seems to me that, contrary to the observations made by Lenin in his time, imperialism is today more concerned with trading with the Third World than investing capital in underdeveloped countries. I repeat that imperialism *cannot do without* many of the basic products and raw materials of the underdeveloped countries and whether they are produced by imperialist enterprises or those of the producing country has become a secondary matter. Moreover, a whole range of techniques has been developed to give imperialism access to such products without necessarily exercising owner-management at the source. Neither can imperialism do without its sales to the Third World which provide almost one quarter of its total exports. At the risk of becoming boring I repeat that such investments as are still made in the secondary industries of the Third World are determined solely by market considerations. If it were always possible to keep a safe hold on markets already conquered and acquire new ones, solely with the products of its own undertakings in the metropolitan countries, imperialism would operate in this way and neglect the industries of the Third World even more than it does at present. What then is the outlet for the capital accumulated in the industrialized countries? Is not imperialism hastening to its doom by reinvesting mainly in the metropolitan countries, and how can one reconcile all this with the classical Marxist theses of reproduction and realization?

It has been seen that decolonization has been followed by stagnation or very slow growth in the absolute value of private investment flowing from imperialist countries to the Third World. Moreover, there has been a decline in the relative value of such investment; the direct and indirect profits from current and older investment, though difficult to evaluate because of all kinds of illegal transfers, are now certainly greater than new investments. In 1965 dividends legally transferred and the servicing of public debts were worth more than all public donations and loans going to the Third World. It is, therefore, reasonable to suggest that a stage has now been reached in which the Third World is far from being a privileged outlet for surplus capital accumulated in the imperialist countries and it is itself beginning to contribute to the surplus.

Hamza Alavi appears to me correct when he says: "The export of capital has not been the principal factor in maintaining the dynamics of post-war capitalism." He refers to a passage from Lenin which has received, perhaps, too little attention:

Twenty years before he wrote his book on imperialism Lenin had been involved in a debate with the populists on the very question of the possibility of the 'internal expansion' of capitalism. He pointed out that it is possible for the internal market to develop in spite of limited consumption by the masses (or in spite of the absence of external outlets). This can happen because, in order to develop production (to accumulate in the strict sense of the term), it is necessary first to produce the means of production. To this end it is necessary to develop the social sector of production which manufactures the means of production and to attract to it workers who are thereby enabled to create a demand for consumer goods. It follows that this consumption appears after accumulation has taken place. Lenin suggests that in this way the accumulated surplus could be absorbed up to a certain point through a relatively rapid expansion of the sector producing capital goods. This would be no more than a respite for capitalism since, in the last resort, productive capacity can only be expanded on the limited basis of consumption. We can see, however, that Lenin visualized two forms of capitalist expansion: the *internal* expansion of capitalism through the relative expansion of the sector producing capital goods and the *external* expansion of capitalism through the export of capital.

It is possible that we are in a period (or nearing its end) during which it has been possible for capitalism to develop by internal expansion through the relatively rapid growth of the sector producing capital goods. One is inclined to think that this is so. Among the factors contributing to the postponement of the crisis, Hamza Alavi mentions:

(a) Public expenditure on the social services and state investment especially in armaments.

(b) The investments of nationalized enterprises.

(c) The effect of the post-war technological revolution and the relative expansion of the sector producing capital goods, both the latter stimulated by the first two factors.

I would add to this list large-scale post-war reconstruction throughout Western Europe and the fact that it was contemporary with the technological revolution. Because these two occurred together the new was greater in scale and better in quality than the old which it replaced. Recent scientific and technological advances have made it possible not merely to replace what had been destroyed by war but to build a new structure. Moreover, force of example has led to modernization and transformation even where the old has not been entirely destroyed. Hence the post-war "miracles" — the German "miracle" and the Italian "miracle" — which are now beginning to look less miraculous. Almost everywhere tensions are appearing; they are not serious as yet but one might say that they are disturbing.

Such tensions appear at the time when the transfer to the Third World of the surplus capital accumulated in the imperialist countries is at such a low ebb that amounts transferred from the Third World exceed new investments flowing to it. Such transfers themselves contribute to accumulation in the capitalist metropolitan countries. Will the disturbing symptoms referred to lead to a reversal of the trend I have described? Will imperialist capital again flow to the underdeveloped countries on a large scale?

I do not think so. The infrastructure required for the pillage of the Third World is, in the main, complete; investments in oil and minerals are not made to order. Above all, the Third World is stirring and available capital is affected by "lack of confidence." The very threat of the great revolution to come in the Third World weighs heavily against the use of this capital. Methods of stimulating investment in underdeveloped countries and ways of insuring against political risks thought up by Western governments have both proved pretty ineffectual in practice.

May it then be supposed that the crisis of reproduction and realization is under way or close at hand and that the symptoms of the collapse or, at least, the slow decay of capitalism can already be discerned? I would be very cautious about making such an assertion but even more so about rejecting it out of hand. More elaborate investigations and data more accessible for collective study would be necessary in order to move toward a conclusion. Even if imperialism has not suffered serious internal contradictions during the recent very propitious period it has not, on the other hand, been able to eliminate all danger of internal contradictions which are inherent in its very nature and always ready to become manifest in suitable conditions. It appears to me that, to say the least, one can say that there is as yet no reason to abandon belief in a general crisis of capitalism — be it catastrophic or slow to develop. It is most likely to appear when the great revolution in the Third World passes from latency to reality for I see in it the most important condition for the exposure of those contradictions latent within the imperialist system.

In his analysis of imperialism Lenin also emphasized that "international monopoly combines of capitalists are formed which divide up the world." "The epoch of the newest capitalism," he writes, "shows us that certain relations are being established between capitalist combines, based on the economic division of the world; while parallel with this and in connection with it, certain relations are being established between political alliances, between states, on the basis of the territorial division of the world, of the struggle for colonies, of the 'struggle for economic territory.'" — Chapter V. For him the new imperialism differs from the old "in substituting for the ambition of a single growing empire the theory and practice of competing empires, each motivated by similar lusts of political aggrandizement and commercial gain." — Chapter VII.

Need I emphasize that this picture, which was so accurate in Lenin's day, no longer reflects the facts of the present? In the first place, formal decolonization is an accomplished fact almost everywhere; on the other hand, mechanical anti-imperialists are mistaken when they insist that neo-colonialism has simply donned the armor of imperialism, that the franc zone is no more than a new name for the French Empire, that the Commonwealth or sterling area is simply the British Empire in a new guise and that each imperialist country has its great overseas preserves and private hunting-grounds as in the past.

There is no doubt that preferential zones continue to exist, as do special links with the former metropolitan imperialist countries which know very well how to preserve as many as possible of their commercial advantages in the former colonies and dependencies by retaining, or dropping, bilateral aid and by using special prices, customs privileges, or guaranteed purchases as instruments of blackmail. We have seen that the former metropolitan country is nearly always the principal trading partner of the 'neo-independent' nation.

However, we have also seen that, in almost every case, even if the relationship of principal trading partner is preserved, it is declining in importance. There is hardly a newly independent state that does not want to diversify its trade channels and most have met with definite, if modest, success in this field. We have found a general tendency for bilateral aid to be relatively reduced and for a relative expansion of international public aid. During the imperialist period it was extremely unusual for any enterprise which was not French to be set up in any territory of the French Empire. Only French enterprises were established under the protection of the tricolored flag. Today the contrary frequently occurs in the franc zone. It is also common for international capital to unite in a single investment. When Simca and Fiat combine with local capital to set up a very artificial assembly plant in Morocco, what state is the power behind the scene? As far as I can tell, two or three were involved, as well as Morocco itself.

It is significant that this tendency usually meets with the approval of the rulers of the imperialist countries, except where certain unavoidable rivalries affect the situation. The Convention associating 18 African countries with the Common Market is characteristic of this trend. At the time of its inception I wrote of imperialism now operating as a cooperative or a limited liability company. Nearly all imperialist governments are ready to give international public aid preference over bilateral aid. At the recent world trade conference in Geneva, did one not hear the British representative declare his country ready to extend to all underdeveloped countries the preference which Britain now accords to those associated with her, on condition that other industrial nations would do the same?

Not so long ago the following equation would have been valid even if rather broad and general: imperialism = United States + Great Britain + France + a few others to pick up the crumbs. Imperialism was the active expression of national capitalist systems embodied in nation states. But direct preferences for a single metropolitan country are crumbling or becoming dissipated in wider arrangements, the trade relations of the imperialist countries are becoming more widespread, and their capital is becoming associated and intermingled as never before. For the Third World, imperialist exploitation tends to become depersonalized and multilateral; it is less often operated through the medium of national capitalist groups and more often through the operation of international, cosmopolitan monopolies increasingly dominated by United States capital.

This is, however, a slow development and we must not go too fast. As yet the tendency I have stressed may be slight, but I believe that it will become more marked because it reflects a new world situation.

Until the advent of the socialist states and even between the wars when the Soviet Union stood alone, the picture painted by Lenin remained accurate. But as China came on the scene after the Second World War more than a third of the world's inhabitants were cut out of the imperialist world market. Whatever may be said to the contrary, the socialist camp remains united on fundamentals and is developing more quickly than the imperialist countries in spite of some fumbling and errors. To this factor we must add the great gale of decolonization. Although it is more formal than real in most places, it would be as foolish to underestimate its importance as to exaggerate it. Even formal independence is a portent and the Third World is heavy with latent storms which are already breaking out here and there. The intoxication of triumphant national liberation is followed by the real picture of exploitation which has not been altered by the drums of victory. Beneath the ethnic and tribal differences which are constantly being rammed down our throats, the outlines of the class struggle appear all the more quickly because the weak ruling class which has taken over has almost always allied itself with imperialism. Specific local conditions derived from the past may partly conceal these class struggles and they certainly do not mature as if by magic. But they are maturing, rapidly or slowly, and, however feeble as yet, they are the true reality of the present and the key to the events of the future.

As the Third World quakes here and there beneath its feet, imperialism becomes doubtful of its own permanence. Exploitation is as ferocious as ever as imperialism seeks to maximize its profits while it can. Faced with a third of the world's people organized in a socialist system, imperialism understands that to organize itself is a condition of its survival and that unity is its temporary safeguard. The division of the world into rival "spheres of influence" shared out between "large monopolistic groupings" which was observed by Lenin has now become risky. In a contracting and tottering world, rivalry among imperialist powers must be moderated and imperialist cohesion established. (The World Bank, International Development Association, Finance Corporation and the like are only the other side of the coin of NATO, SEATO and similar pacts, to say nothing of the Organization of American States.) President Kennedy knew what he was talking about when he stated that the purpose of international aid was to "defend the frontiers of the free world everywhere." Certainly internal rivalries do not disappear at the wave of a wand and the eddies of change are often concealed beneath the surface. In the end, events are determined by the capital and policies of Wall Street because they are the strongest. Imperialism as a single world system is finding it necessary to manifest itself as such everywhere, but more especially in the Third World. No more special preserves for segments of imperialism, no more secondary confrontations; but, as long as it can be maintained, one great happy hunting ground: the whole Third World for a single, united, complete imperialism.

I do not deny that at the present moment this picture may seem exaggerated. It is, however, correct when it is presented as that of a new reality, hard to discern as yet, but pushing its way to the present. I would not have attached so much importance to certain signs had they appeared to be isolated, and still less if they had been in conflict with each other. My investigations, on the contrary, revealed a pattern: a tendency to increasing internationalization of trade with the Third World, of aid to the Third World, and of private investment in the Third World; an overall tendency to the increasing internationalization of contractual and treaty arrangements with the Third World. Separately, these trends are still weak, but their congruity seems to be significant. It suggests a new form of imperialist action, adapted to a new world situation, but making no real change in the basic motives or essential character of imperialism. It has now been established that two features of imperialism as Lenin saw it no longer characterize the system. Must one conclude that Lenin is out of date?

The emphasis placed by Lenin upon the export of capital in his period served only to illuminate his theory of the tribute levied by imperialism from the underdeveloped countries. The existence of this tribute has been observed at every turn; it is only the method of levying it which has changed with the new conditions. Today this tribute has become so heavy that it exceeds new investment and, instead of being a recipient of the surplus of capital accumulation, the Third World is now itself taking part in it.

Similarly, it appeared to Lenin that the division of the world among the great powers and the international cartels were only the means appropriate to the time for bringing all the sources of primary raw materials under imperialist control. Has the imperialism of the 1960's abandoned such control or the pillage of the Third World? It has perforce to use different methods — that is all. It has adapted itself but without losing its essential nature which, through the new modes of action, remains exactly as Lenin defined it.

Those who want to revise or relegate Lenin to the past also make out that he was mistaken in foreseeing an early and apocalyptic end to imperialism. Because this has not come about, discredit is supposed to fall on a whole body of theory on which unfulfilled predictions are said to rest. Lenin described imperialism as "capitalism in transition," or, more precisely, as "dying capitalism." — *Imperialism,* Chapter X. It is said ironically that "it is a slow death-agony." But Lenin never claimed to have laid down a time-table for the world revolution. Having described imperialism as "parasitic or decaying capitalism," he hastened to add: "It would be a mistake to believe that this tendency to decay precludes a rapid growth of capitalism" and, later, "as a whole, capitalism is growing far more rapidly than before" and he concludes: "Private business relations, and private property relations, constitute a shell which is no longer suitable to the contents, a shell which must inevitably begin to decay if its removal is postponed by artificial means; a shell which may continue in a state of decay for a comparatively long period (particularly if the cure of the opportunist abscess is protracted), but which will inevitably be removed."

Far from claiming to revise or relegate Lenin to the past, I prefer to stand on his ground as far as I am able, and to follow his line of thought. It is in this spirit that I have laid bare certain new features of imperialism in the 1960's and now think it worth while to consider the consequences which might flow from them both for the nations of the Third World and for the anti-capitalist groupings inside the capitalist countries.

Many will regard it as platitudinous to assert that the countries of the Third World can only escape from imperialist exploitation by the socialist road. But does not daily experience show that what one took to be a platitude still requires exposition? All sorts of illusions are more persistent than one had imagined — and not only in the Third World. Some believe that one must make the best use one can of imperialism while condemning it, or that one must run with the hounds and that there are some positive values in imperialism; others that capitalist imperialism has overcome its major contradictions and is now developing harmoniously and, since socialism is so difficult to establish, one must willy-nilly find a *modus vivendi* with imperialism and try to make the best one can of it.

I think this investigation has shown that for the Third World in particular, there is no hope of ending exploitation and underdevelopment within the framework of the imperialist system. The Indian situation alone is a tragic illustration which is so often, and so rightly, referred to that it need not be recapitulated here. The most important conclusion to be drawn from this analysis is the belief, not only that imperialism persists unchanged in its essential nature, but also, and most emphatically, that the exploitation and underdevelopment which it causes are growing more severe. Seventy or eighty countries of the Third World may indeed be the "peers" of the "great powers" of the Western world in majestic international proceedings; their representatives may receive flattering marks of high esteem, be entrusted with the chairman's gavel and be met at airports in grand style — but the others are still the pillagers and they are still the pillaged, more and more as time passes.

The peoples of the Third World extract ever more basic materials, minerals, and primary products and for these the imperialist buyers pay less and less. In return the people of the Third World are obliged to buy more and more of the manufactured goods they lack and, as these goods increase in price, and their income from exports falls, they have to cut back on their essential needs or else extract a larger volume of basic products the price of which then falls further; there is no way out for them. In 1935 the standard of living of the citizens of the United States was 17 times that of the Indians; in 1962 it was 35 times higher. During the last ten years economic growth has continued to increase faster in the imperialist countries than in the Third World. As Lenin had already observed: "Finance capital and the trusts are aggravating instead of diminishing the differences between the rates of development of the various parts of the world economy." — *Imperialism,* Chapter VII.

There is really no way out for the people of the Third World in this context. It is not a question of whether socialism is attractive to their rulers or leading thinkers; it would be dishonest to conceal from them that the first stage of socialism is not a bed of roses, and that it is not built in one day with banners waving. It is simply a matter of accepting the evidence: there *is* no other possible solution; like it or not, for them China is the great example.

At this point I must make it clear that it is not a question of just any kind of socialism. Few words, few ideas, have been so misused but only one socialism has conquered hunger and, whatever the pundits of idealism may say, only one socialism has made slaves into men, and that is the socialism of Marx and Lenin.

It is not a matter of imitating anyone along this road but only of taking inspiration from the best examples. It is for the peoples of the Third World alone to find the roads they will take to socialism and for my part I will conclude our study only by underlining a few facts and indicating some lines of thought which may be of value to this end.

First, it should never be forgotten that however heavily imperialist exploitation weighs on the Third World this exploitation needs the Third World and cannot do without it. In the course of this analysis it has been shown that the Third World is the sole or principal source of many products or raw materials without which many of the markets of imperialism would collapse and many of its most essential factories come to a standstill. The significance of this is heightened by reading a report recently prepared by a group of French research workers under the title "Reflections for 1985."[2] Concerning itself especially with data having a bearing on the future, the report sets out to determine what will be the essential needs of the French economy in certain fields, twenty years from now.

With regard to minerals, the authors establish that French need might be multiplied by 2.5 but that French production would then stand at an index of only 0.7 or 0.8 of the 1961 level, the decrease being the result of exhaustion. An examination of the prospects for

---

[2] *La Documentation Française,* November, 1964.

Europe as a whole leads to the expectation of increasing shortages. The report examines the position regarding all the major products and shows that France is entirely dependent on imports for oil, copper, lead, zinc, manganese, and phosphates, and heavily so for iron, bauxite, sulphur, and pyrites. It concludes: "It certainly seems that the French economy must prepare for an increasing drain on its balance of payments to meet its needs in minerals. In 1961 such imports amounted to two fifths of her needs; in 1985 they might amount to four fifths; between 1961 and 1985 they will be multiplied by about 5 (in 1961 francs). The economy of Europe as a whole will find itself in the same position."

The report ends with the comment: "Such heavy dependence on international resources cannot but influence the long-term orientation of French and European foreign policy." I think one can add that such heavy dependence can have an objective effect upon the policies of the Third World. For, as we saw in Chapter II, most of these "international resources" are in the hands of the Third World. In this study I have stressed the tendency in the Third World for national capitalist systems supported by particular imperialist states to be replaced by international oligarchies seeking to control major markets and sources of raw materials, not to mention the great international industrial complexes which try to ensure for themselves access to sources of raw material by vertical integration. It has also been emphasized that while, on the one hand, the increasing volume of trade between imperialist countries is less and less concerned with essential goods there is, on the other hand, nothing inessential or marginal involved in the trade between the Third World and the imperialist countries. It is all in basic essentials and "Reflections for 1985" suggests that these characteristics apply to Europe's trade in minerals and will do so more and more.

Do these facts and prospects not suggest that the countries of the Third World could make the most of the fact that they hold the sources of indispensable raw materials by embarking on a policy of economic 'united fronts' rather than allowing themselves to become engulfed in purposeless 'common markets'? For some 20 years the well-meaning personnel of the U.N. have vainly attempted to organize the markets in basic products but the imperialist nations may one day undertake to do so for their own benefit when it suits their strategy. If the nations of the Third World have the will they can organize such markets unilaterally and for their common benefit. They can get a little something out of imperialism in a number of basic sectors and make their own wealth enrich *them* just a little until it is turned entirely to this purpose when they themselves transform it into a socialist economic system.

Until the countries of the Third World take to the hard road that leads to socialism they are condemned to live on whatever terms they can with the imperialism which despoils them but, for that very reason, cannot do without them. The relations between the Third World and imperialism are dialectical and not all the weapons are on one side.

I have made a pretty fierce analysis of imperialism in the various sectors into which it can be divided. But my analysis is fierce only because, wherever I look, I find ferocity under the screen of figures. There is surely no need to reconsider this: one cannot take a share in imperialism or build a future on compromise with it. Does this mean, however, that no provisional arrangement is ever possible, that one must submit totally to imperialism or reject it in toto even in a transitional period? To take an absolutist stand on this point implies ignorance of the fact that the Third World and the imperialist countries are reciprocally enmeshed and of the dialectical nature of their reciprocal relations. Among the things I have condemned are so-called imperialist aid and association with the European Common Market: does this mean that *all* aid must be rejected in all circumstances and that *any* contract with the Common Market (other than association) must always be turned down? By definition one bargains with an enemy; there is no need to do so with a friend, and Marxists have never excluded compromises. There is one condition: that a compromise should not be seen as an end but as a stage, not as an outcome but as a breathing space; it should be a tactical phase and not the purpose of a strategy.

The aridity and complexity of figures and the facts derived from them reveal partial truths which converge toward a general truth. I wanted to give priority to the facts and figures because of the significance of their witness. The real face of imperialism is revealed without adornment in columns of figures and one must reject the temptation to look beyond them for other lessons. This work would be of little value to anyone who had skimmed the figures and analysis with half an eye and there is no need for elaboration for those who have immersed themselves in them. For them, I hope, conviction has been carried and personal reflection will do the rest, and that is all that I hoped to induce in my readers. I do, however, wish to direct a word to the anti-capitalists of the imperialist countries and especially of Europe. Lenin often expresses the idea that imperialism "which means monopolistically high profits for a handful of very rich countries, creates the economic possibility of corrupting the upper strata of the proletariat, and thereby fosters, gives form to, and strengthens opportunism." — *Imperialism,* Chapter VIII. He also says: "The imperialist ideology is also permeating the working class. There is no Chinese wall between it and the other classes." — Chapter IX. This thesis, so strongly held by Lenin, is recalled to one's mind by a proliferation of Western European works and articles by unofficial, and sometimes even by official spokesmen of progressive, working-class, and Marxist trends. These purport to concern themselves with the present problems of the working class and the way to socialism and almost all have the following in common:

(a) The Third World and the great struggle already under way between it and imperialism goes unmentioned. The implicit basic postulate is that Western capitalism has already achieved stability and found organizational forms which put it beyond the reach of any major general crisis. The argument is conducted as if capitalism existed only in Europe and North America.

(b) It follows that a basic Marxist-Leninist thesis is abandoned without any discussion: the thesis that the imperialist stage of capitalism is its most developed, and its last, and that the growing contradiction between the development and concentration of the forces of production on the one hand and capitalist relations of production on the other will ring the death knell of capitalism. This does not mean, of course, that capitalism will end in 1975 or 1990.

(c) In this context socialism is not presented as the superior system which must, and which alone can, succeed capitalism (which does not mean that there is no more to be done than sit by with folded hands). Socialism is presented simply as a possible, but not a necessary, alternative; and consequently the intensification of the class struggle is abandoned in an effort to carry conviction that socialism is "preferable."

Many of the articles and works nevertheless have value, provide correct partial analyses and lucid critiques of particular aspects of contemporary capitalism — for instance the new forms of alienation in the so-called affluent society. But such work is in basic error and is the intellectual offspring of an opportunist trend fostered by the relative and contingent prosperity of capitalism during the last 15 years.

An analysis of present-day capitalism should not be limited to the features it exhibits in highly industrialized countries. Such a narrow view ignores the fact that imperialism is, more than ever, a world-wide system nourishing the prosperity of the metropolitan countries with tribute pillaged from the Third World and that the working class of the industrial countries is objectively a minor partner in this exploitation even while being itself exploited by imperialism.

Some very simple questions must be posed:

Is it to be assumed that the present international division of labor is permanent? That the Third World will not become aware and awake whatever the timing and the manner of its awakening may be?

If an affirmative reply is given to the first question, is it to be supposed that the emancipation of the Third World will not strike a death blow at imperialism? While it is being undermined at the base, will the relation of world forces not be radically altered so that even the champions of peaceful competition between East and West must perceive the unlimited perspective that will at last be open for the socialist East?

Does not this show that the hackneyed argument as to whether the fundamental contradiction of our time is between socialism and capitalism or between imperialism and the Third World is badly formulated? Since the emancipation of the Third World can only come when it takes the socialist road, the first contradiction will disappear when the second is resolved and who would suggest, as matters stand in the world today, that this is not extremely likely to be the order of events? Though the contradiction between capitalism and socialism seems to be essential and fundamental in present conditions, it is concretely subordinate to the resolution of the contradiction between imperialism and the Third World.

If this is accepted it surely follows that all aid to the revolutionary movements of the Third World in their struggle for emancipation is the most urgent and decisive task. Even if the accession of representatives of the Western working class to positions of power is a correct demand (I see it as reformist in character), is it not right to see it in perspective? It is right that everyone should devote himself to making the revolution at home in the most appropriate way but international solidarity must not be an empty phrase and should surely be exercised most forcefully where the enemy appears to be most vulnerable: that is, in the Third World.

MONTHLY REVIEW

an independent socialist magazine
edited by Paul M. Sweezy and Harry Magdoff

Business Week: ". . . a brand of socialism that is thorough-going and tough-minded, drastic enough to provide the sharp break with the past that many left-wingers in the underdeveloped countries see as essential. At the same time they maintain a sturdy independence of both Moscow and Peking that appeals to neutralists. And their skill in manipulating the abstruse concepts of modern economics impresses would-be intellectuals. . . . Their analysis of the troubles of capitalism is just plausible enough to be disturbing."

Bertrand Russell: "Your journal has been of the greatest interest to me over a period of time. I am not a Marxist by any means as I have sought to show in critiques published in several books, but I recognize the power of much of your own analysis and where I disagree I find your journal valuable and of stimulating importance. I want to thank you for your work and to tell you of my appreciation of it."

The Wellesley Department of Economics: " . . . the leading Marxist intellectual (not Communist) economic journal published anywhere in the world, and is on our subscription list at the College library for good reasons."

Albert Einstein: "Clarity about the aims and problems of socialism is of greatest significance in our age of transition. . . . I consider the founding of this magazine to be an important public service." (In his article, "Why Socialism" in Vol. I, No. 1.)

DOMESTIC: $9 for one year, $16 for two years, $7 for one-year student subscription.

FOREIGN: $10 for one year, $18 for two years, $8 for one-year student subscription. (Subscription rates subject to change.)

116 West 14th Street, New York, New York 10011